LOWER BEBINGTON'S
FALLEN
1914 – 1919

A Sacrifice Supreme

by

Dave Horne

COUNTYVISE LTD

First Published 2013 by Countyvise Ltd
14 Appin Road, Birkenhead, CH41 9HH

British Library Cataloguing in Publication Data.
A catalogue record for this book is available from the British Library.

ISBN 978 1 906823 89 4

This book is dedicated to my inspiration:

WILLIAM HORNE - 1st Royal Dragoons
died 1st September 1916
from wounds received at Ovillers, Somme.

CONTENTS

FOREWORD

THIS BOOK TELLS THE STORY of the men named on the Memorial Tablet inside St. Andrew's Church, Lower Bebington.

Having had such a rewarding time producing my first book in 2012, I found it impossible not to attempt just one more book. After all there are two Bebingtons!

This time it is the story of the men from Lower Bebington who gave their lives in the Great War. I say 'attempt' because there are 73 names on this memorial and it has been a big undertaking. The actual research is at least 75% of the work and it needs to be done with the proverbial fine toothcomb in order not to miss the slightest clue that might help to find the story behind any particular name on the memorial tablet.

The writing part doesn't come any easier to me either, and I apologise once again for my lack of literary skills. This is not a grumble on my part though, because the satisfaction of finding out what these men did for their country far outweighs any of the hard work involved.

What is most important is that these brave men from our town are remembered for their sacrifice all those years ago. The majority of them volunteered immediately, or in the first few months of the war, and many of them left behind a wife and children.

The men are not discussed in any particular order, alphabetical or otherwise. Several are brothers, some were in the same Battalion, and some died on the same day or in the same battle, so I have tried to group these together if possible in the hope that it all becomes a more 'joined up' story of Lower Bebington's Fallen. I have also used the men's full Christian names (i.e. Frederick, not Fred) unless I know for sure that they were known to their family by a shorter version.

Almost all of the Higher Bebington men tended to be locals born and bred, in what was a very small and separate community all those years ago. Lower Bebington is a different story, in the 1890's and early 1900's there was an influx of people from other parts of Cheshire, North Shropshire, and even parts of Lancashire. A lot of them had been attracted by the success of the Lever Brothers factory in Port Sunlight, which provided secure employment, a company house, and an attractive environment.

Consequently it is noticeable that many of the soldiers in this book were either born outside the area or born locally to parents from further afield.

It is also worth noting that the Higher Bebington boundary was very easy to define, and apart from an area called Woodhey at the bottom of Town Lane that was often referred to at the time as Rock Ferry, Higher Bebington was - Higher Bebington.

Lower Bebington on the other hand, at least as far as the memorial is concerned, seemed to adopt the nearby townships of Port Sunlight, New Ferry and even Bromborough Pool to some extent. When the memorial was being planned in the early 1920's all the local people had been asked to supply the names of servicemen who had lost their lives, so if the parents or wife of one of the casualties didn't respond then they probably didn't go on it.

On the other hand, it would seem to be the case that if a mother from Bromborough Pool wanted her son on the memorial then they only had to ask. This is not a criticism at all, just my idea as to why some casualties from New Ferry & Port Sunlight are named and yet many others are not.

It has to be emphasised that the Lower Bebington memorial is certainly not a definitive list of all the men from the district who gave their lives in the war, but 73 is certainly enough for my purposes. After all, this book is written about the men who ARE named on the memorial!

It does occur to me though that whilst Port Sunlight and Bromborough Pool do also have their own memorials, with names, it is a shame that New Ferry does not. St. Mark's church has a nice memorial cross but there are no names on it, or on a tablet inside the church.

Finally, by way of an advertisement, if any reader should want a copy of my previous book then would they please contact me on the phone number given at the back of the book. I can arrange for free delivery, and gladly sign it if required!

Equally if any reader should want some help or advice regarding other local men who served in the Great War, including the lucky ones who came home, then they should feel free to ask. If I don't know the answer then I may well know someone who does.

Dave Horne – October 2013.

THE MEMORIAL CROSS

Seemingly designed never to catch the sun!
This photograph was taken on a Saturday evening in early July just as
the last of the days sunshine was catching it.

THE BASE OF THE MEMORIAL CROSS

The inscriptions on the front and back faces of the base.

THE MEMORIAL CROSS IS CARVED out of Darley Dale stone and was made locally at David McGivering's Monumental Works, 15 Town Lane, Bebington.

The inscriptions at the base, which were a subject of much discussion at the committee meetings in the early 1920's, were done by Earp, Hobbs and Miller of Lower Mosley Street, Manchester.

iv

THE MEMORIAL TABLET

Made in Oak, by Harry Hems & sons of Exeter (see transcription)

THE NAMES OF THE FALLEN

A PHOTOGRAPH OF THE MEMORIAL tablet is shown on the previous page, but it is difficult to get a clear enough image for it to be easily read in this book, so the exact transcription given below should make things clearer.

TO THE GLORY OF GOD AND IN GRATEFUL MEMORY

J. NORMAN AUSTIN	WILLIAM FORSEY	GEORGE J. POWYS
ERNEST BARCLAY	THOMAS H. GATES	RICHARD J. E. RYCROFT
WILLIAM BRAYNE	JOHN GEE	GEORGE SCHEERS
HERBERT A. BROWN	HARRY GEORGE	FRANK J. SCHENKEL
WILLIAM A. BROWN	ROLAND GREEN	WILLIAM SPARK
RALPH R. BROCKLEBANK	JAMES GRIFFITHS	JOHN STATHAM
GEORGE R. COATHUP	FREDERICK HARDWICK	HENRY SMEDLEY
GEORGE COOPER	HORACE HOLDEN	WALTER J. SEVERN
ARTHUR DAVIES	JOHN M. HULL	BASIL H. STEELE
ERIC DAVIES	MICHAEL HUNT	ERNEST SMITH
FRANK A. DAVIES	HENRY V. HUGHES	FRANK SMITH
REGINALD E. DAVIES	GEORGE F. INSKIP	P. JAMES SMITH
HENRY DAVIES M.M.	E. JAMES IVESON	RICHARD P. SCHOLEFIELD
JOHN DAWBER	JOSEPH JONES	PHILIP SHONE
ARNOLD I. DRAPER	PERCY D. KENDALL	W. HERBERT SUCKLEY
FREDERICK DELLOW	SAMUEL LANCASTER	W. ERNEST WATSON D.S.O.
ANDREW DILLON	ERNEST G. LEATHER	JOHN N. WARD
HERBERT DILLON	H. JOHN LEWIS	AARON WHITE M.M.
ALBERT DODD	ARTHUR MARGERISON	GEORGE WHITEHEAD
WALTER DUNN	FRANK MELLOR	RALPH WILLIAMS
JOS. WM. DUTTON	JOSEPH MULLRAY	PERCY WILLIAMS
ALFRED EVANS	ARTHUR NEVITT	HERBERT WILSON
MATTHEW FRAY	RICHARD LeB. NICHOLSON MC	WILLIAM H.WOOLLISCROFT
WILLIAM FITTON M.M.	H. PERCY PARRY	
KENNETH G. H. FORD	J. STANLEY PEARSON	

THIS TABLET RECORDS THE NAMES OF THE MEN WHO DIED IN THE GREAT WAR TO WHOSE HONOUR THE CROSS IN THE CHURCHYARD HAS BEEN ERECTED

Casting a critical eye over the names it should be pointed out that Samuel Lancaster was really Samuel White (see his particular story elsewhere in the book).

Woolliscroft has an extra "L" - according to his birth and marriage certificates it should read Wooliscroft.

Finally the two Smith brothers Ernest and James should ideally have been next to one another, as the four Davies brothers were.

PLANNING & UNVEILING THE MEMORIAL

AFTER SOME INFORMAL DISCUSSIONS HAD taken place, a public meeting was held in the Mayer Hall on Friday 25th February 1921 to discuss the plans for a suitable memorial.

The Rector, Reverend Hugh E. Boultbee took the chair and outlined what appeared to be two proposals, a smaller one with just a memorial tablet inside St. Andrew's church and a larger one which would consist of a memorial tablet with the addition of a stone cross in the new part of the churchyard.

Mr. William Nicholson (a father of one of the fallen) promised a very generous donation of £100 if the larger scheme were to be adopted and Mrs. Constance Brocklebank (a mother of one of the fallen) also strongly supported the larger scheme.

After a discussion the two proposals were put to the vote and the bigger scheme was carried with a *"very large majority"*.

A committee was duly elected to go into the necessary details and carry out the approved scheme.

There were many and regular meetings, occasionally twice a month, and they carried on throughout 1921, 1922 and 1923. Collections were organised to raise the necessary funds, and at a meeting in the Drill Hall on 11th August 1921 it was reported that over £316 had already been received and another £213 had been promised. Members of the public had previously been asked to submit names of the fallen and, somewhat surprisingly at this point in time, only 20 had been received. At the same meeting it was also reported that the Wesleyan Chapel in Bromborough Road would like to use the same names as St.Andrews on their own memorial tablet and the committee offered them help if required.

At a meeting in the Vestry on Sunday 26th November 1922 it was revealed that the names of the fallen now totalled 60. There was to be a final appeal in the church and also in the shops in the village and then the list would be closed on December 16th.

By April 8th 1923 the meetings were still going strong and the inscriptions at the base of the memorial cross were finally decided upon. At around the same time estimates were asked for engraving the names of the fallen on the Tablet, quotes were provided for name only, or name and rank. Unsurprisingly the committee decided on the cheaper option.

The memorials in Higher Bebington, Port Sunlight, and New Ferry had all been completed by December 1921, and letters expressing concern about the lack of progress were written to the Architects but eventually an unveiling date for the Memorial was set for Sunday October 14th 1923 and Lord Leverhulme, no less, was asked to do the unveiling - only for him to cancel as late as September 23rd.

The Bishop of Chester had also agreed to attend the unveiling, but on the proviso that the committee could *"bring him from Heswall and motor him back to Chester"*!

The big day finally arrived, after nearly three years in the planning.

It was a Sunday afternoon and the *"Birkenhead News"* and *"Birkenhead Advertiser"* gave excellent coverage in the following Saturday editions.

There was a muted peal of the church bells for ten minutes before the procession started from the District Council Offices. It was led by the Band of the 4/5th Cheshire Regiment, followed by Council members, Ex-servicemen, Port Sunlight Fire Brigade, the Church Lads Brigade, Girl Guides, and the Police.

A crowd of between 1,000 and 2,000 had assembled at the memorial, with relatives of the fallen being placed in prominent positions. The Bishop of Chester Dr. H. L. Paget accompanied by his Chaplain Rev. H. A. Bull, the Rev. J.W. Faraday from the Wesleyan Chapel, and Rev. H. E. Boultbee the Rector of Bebington then proceeded to the memorial which was draped with Union Jacks.

Thanks are given to the Birkenhead News for permission to use the above photograph.

THE CEREMONY COMMENCED WITH THE singing of "O God, our help in ages past" accompanied by the Band of the Cheshires. This was followed by the Lord's Prayer, and after delivering a short address Mr. John Barber J.P. (Chairman of the Bebington & Bromborough U.D.C.) unveiled and dedicated the memorial.

Kipling's Recessional was sung by the choir, and the Benediction Prayer was pronounced by the Bishop of Chester after which a bugler sounded "The Last Post". Two minutes silence were observed, followed by "Reveille".

The Band played Beethoven's Funeral March, during which many beautiful wreaths were laid at the foot of the Memorial Cross. The outside ceremony finished with the National Anthem.

Many of those in attendance then proceeded into the church for the unveiling of the Memorial Tablet by the Bishop. A religious service was held first, including an address by the Bishop before he pulled aside the flag draped over the tablet.

Later in the evening the Wesleyan brass Memorial Tablet was also unveiled by Mr. John Barber before a large congregation.

By 16th February 1925 the project was finally completed when the accounts were audited. Having raised the necessary funds of just over £689 (plus some bank interest) by public subscription, the major costs had worked out as follows :

The Memorial Cross by D.McGivering, Monumental Works, Town Lane, Bebington. - £400

Engraving of the base of the Cross   by Earp, Hobbs and Miller of Manchester - £56-16s

The Oak Tablet by Harry Hems & Sons of Exeter - £97-3s-6d

The Brass Tablet (Wesleyan Chapel) by Gilkes' of Reading. £50

Architects fees   C.E. Deacon & Son, Liverpool. - £55-6s

The remainder of the cost, amounting to about £48, was for miscellaneous items including : Labour, Shrubs, Draining, and Printing.

Apologies are offered to those readers who don't remember the days of £.s.d ! (pounds, shillings, and pence)

CAMPAIGN MEDALS

THE STANDARD CAMPAIGN MEDALS ISSUED for service in the Great War were the 1914 Star or 1914/15 Star, the British War Medal, and the Victory Medal.

The 1914 Star (also known as the Mons Star) was awarded to officers and men who served in France or Belgium between August 5th and midnight on the 22nd/23rd of November 1914.
The 1914/15 Star was awarded to officers and men of British and Imperial forces who served in any theatre of the War between the 5th August 1914 and 31st December 1915 (but not to those who had already qualified for the 1914 Star).

The British War Medal was awarded to officers and men of British and Imperial forces who served anywhere overseas between the 5th August 1914 and 11th November 1918.

The Victory Medal was awarded to officers and men who entered a theatre of war between 5 August 1914 and 11 November 1918, it was never awarded on its own.

Most of the 73 men on the Lower Bebington Memorial only received 1, 2 or 3 of these medals (and two men would not have received any) However, one man was awarded a Military Cross + Bar and three of the men were awarded a Military Medal. These medals are pictured with each mans story.

| 1914 Star | 1914/15 Star | British War Medal | Victory Medal |

THE MEMORIAL PLAQUE

MADE OF BRONZE AND 4¾" in diameter, it was sometimes called the Death Plaque or Dead Man's Penny, it is embossed with the name of the serviceman in the rectangular panel, the reverse is completely blank.

Accompanied by a commemorative scroll, it was issued to the next of kin of all British and Commonwealth servicemen and women whose death was attributable to the First World War.

MAP OF BEBINGTON — 1910

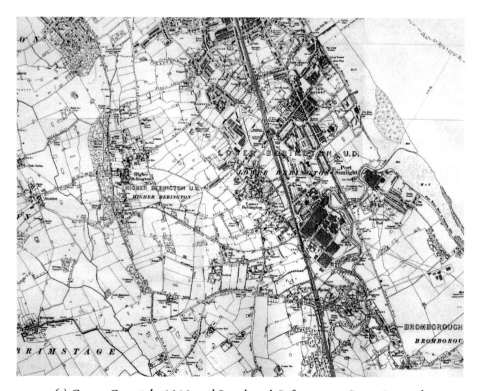

A section from the Ordnance Survey Map of 1910.

NOTE THE RIVER MERSEY TOP right hand corner, and the Birkenhead to Chester railway line running from top to bottom, just right of centre. The Lever Brothers, Port Sunlight and Prices, Bromborough Pool factories are very prominent to the right of the railway line, also the dense housing in New Ferry a bit further north.

Higher Bebington and Storeton are to the left centre and the Poulton-cum-Spital area is at bottom centre.

THE DAVIES BROTHERS – ARTHUR, ERIC, FRANK & REGINALD

THIS IS A TRAGIC TALE INDEED, a family who lost four sons in the Great War.

The parents were William & Maria Davies (nee Johnson), William was born in Bebington and worked in the cotton industry throughout his working life, being listed as a Cotton Salesman on the 1911 census.

The couple were married on 9th April 1879 at St. Nicholas' church in Liverpool, and they had a total of 18 children, all born in Bebington, with 14 of them still surviving at the time of the 1911 census.

The 14 in birth order were : William, John, Florence Evelyn ("Floss"), Arthur, twins Edwin & Elsie, Herbert Leslie, Frank Arnold, Albert Cecil, Reginald Ernest, Beatrice Maud ("Lou"), Eric, Doris Gertrude and Constance Alma. (pause for breath!)

One set of twins survived but another pair, Albert and Amy, died soon after birth. Ethel May was born in 1884 but died aged 3, and young Thomas died the day after he was born.

In 1891 they were living at 26 Bromborough Road, Lower Bebington, in 1901 they had moved to 20 Trafalgar Drive, and by 1911 they were in an 8 roomed house at No. 1 The Village, Lower Bebington. When 3 of the sons volunteered in 1914 the family were living at No.17

The Village. This lovely house is still there today and a photograph is shown here. There is no more than ½ mile covering all four addresses.

After the war, in 1921, the father and some of his children moved again, to "Lynwood" No.20 Higher Bebington Road, still in Lower Bebington though.

1

The *"Birkenhead News"* reported at length on the deaths of the first two sons in 1915 and 1916, but there was nothing at all for the second two. There was actually a very sad reason for this, Maria died on 28th May 1917 aged 59. Family memories are that she died of a broken heart, thankfully she wasn't to know that things were going to go from bad to worse.

A few brief notes about 5 of the sons careers follow :

Arthur Davies : Born second quarter 1887, he never married, and was employed as a Cashier at a Cotton Merchants (presumably Liverpool Cotton Exchange).

Frank Arnold Davies : Born 20th December 1892 and educated at Wallasey Grammar School. A bachelor. He served his time with Messrs. J. Hoult but when he enlisted he was employed as a Shipping Clerk for Messrs. J.M. Edmiston in Exchange Buildings, Liverpool. Frank was a member of Sefton Park Cricket Club and also an enthusiastic footballer.

Reginald Ernest Davies ("Reg") : Born 22nd May 1895. Another bachelor who was employed in the Liverpool office of Bass, Ratcliff & Gretton (Brewers).

Eric Davies : Born 21st September 1897. Little else is known.

Herbert Leslie Davies ("Bert") : Born 2nd November 1891. Worked as a Cotton Salesman before the war and enlisted in the 6th Battalion King's Liverpool Regiment at the same time as Reg and Frank. He was commissioned in the 4th Battalion Cheshires in October 1916, finishing the war as a Lieutenant. Soon after the war he immigrated to the United States and was living at Fort Worth Texas at the time his medals were issued. He later lived at Glendale, California.

The writer has been lucky enough to meet Gwen, the only granddaughter of John, one of the older brothers. She has shared a few family memories with me, and the excellent photographs used in this book were kindly supplied by her. A family photograph of six of the brothers in cricket whites is shown below.

2057 RIFLEMAN REGINALD ERNEST DAVIES
6th Battalion Kings Liverpool Regiment

REG ENLISTED WITH THE "Liverpool Rifles" as they were popularly known, in Liverpool on Monday 31st August 1914. He trained at Merstham in Surrey before moving down the road to Sevenoaks in Kent. His brothers Frank & Bert probably joined the same day (their numbers are pretty close together).

At the time of enlistment he was 19 years 3 months, almost 5'-10" tall, and weighed 11 stone.

After completing their training the Battalion boarded the "S.S. City of Edinburgh" at Southampton on 24th February 1915 and disembarked in France later that day. Reg was accompanied by his two brothers Frank and Bert.

His active service career was to last just over 7 weeks, and the Battalion war diary reported that on Friday 16th April they were settled in billets in Ypres. It was a quiet day, just one man killed and one wounded.

On the Saturday they moved into old casemates in the ramparts of the town, and at 7pm they heard explosions under Hill 60 and were heavily bombarded by German artillery during the night. The following day they remained in reserve at the ramparts, but the diary noted that a ration party lost 1 man killed, 2 men wounded, and 1 mule killed. They also had Companies attached to the Norfolk Regiment and 4 Kingsmen were killed and 4 wounded with them. It looks as though Reg was either the man killed in the ration party or else he was with the Norfolks. He was killed in action on Sunday 18th April 1915 at the age of just 19.

His parents were first informed of his death in a letter from his brother Bert who was also in the same Regiment. At this point in time they had 3 sons in the 6th Kings Liverpool, Reg, Bert and Frank (who transferred to the Cheshires in January 1916). At least two other brothers served in the war, Eric and Arthur. Their stories are told on the following pages.

Reg is buried in Blauwepoort Farm Cemetery, just 2 miles south east of Ypres town centre. It is a very small cemetery with just 82 burials. A photograph is shown on the following page.

Reg qualified for a 1915 Star, British War Medal and Victory Medal.

His father should also have received a Memorial Plaque and Scroll.

2ⁿᴰ LIEUTENANT FRANK ARNOLD DAVIES
6ᵗʰ Battalion Kings Liverpool &
5ᵗʰ Battalion Cheshire Regiment

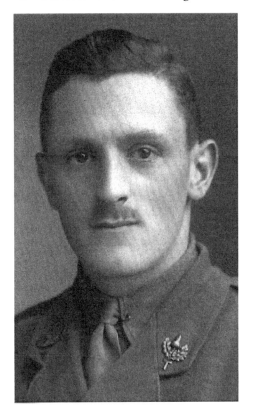

Frank enlisted as 2092 Private Frank Davies with the 6th Kings Liverpool at the outbreak of the war.

His brother Reg enlisted on Monday 31st August and their service numbers are so close together that they probably joined up the same day. Brother Bert also joined the 6th Battalion at this time. After completing their training together the three brothers all boarded the

"S.S. City of Edinburgh" at Southampton on 24th February 1915 and disembarked in France later that day.

A local newspaper reported that Frank had been wounded slightly soon after, but it was nothing serious.

Nothing more can be reported about him until he was offered a commission with the 5th Battalion Cheshire Regiment. He trained with the Inns of Court Officer Training Corps, and became a 2nd Lieutenant in January 1916.

The photograph of him was supplied by a member of the family, and shows him as a 2nd Lieutenant in the 5th Cheshires. The Cheshire badge is on his collars, and the "T" signifies Territorial.

According to the book *"The War Record of the 1/5th (Earl of Chester's) Battalion, The Cheshire Regiment"* by Lieut.Col. W.A.V. Churton, Frank joined his new unit in France on 30th May 1916.

He was killed at Gommecourt on the the first day of the Somme, aged 23. The book gives a graphic account of the action on this day and Frank is mentioned by name twice. Great use of this book is used in the concise version of events given here.

The attack at Gommecourt was a diversionary action designed to draw German reserves from the main British offensive further south.

The 5th Cheshires were a part of 56th Division and their orders that day, in a nutshell, were to capture and clear the village of Gommecourt.

Zero hour was 7.30am and "A" Company of the Cheshires were first over the top but met with little success. Frank and 2nd Lt. W.F. Smith had previously been designated to lead two Platoons from "B" Company to fix name plates in any captured German trenches, and soon after 7.30am they attempted to get across no mans land.

Frank was killed as soon as he mounted the parapet of the trench and *"the fire was so heavy and the situation so doubtful that they were ordered to stand fast"*. The book gives casualty figures just for the 3 Platoons of "B" Company and 1 Platoon of "D" Company of 1 Officer (Frank) and 37 Other Ranks.

Frank's Colonel wrote to his parents – *"I am sorry to say your boy was killed whilst leading his men over the parapet of the trench. He was shot through the head and was killed instantly. He had proved himself a capable officer and his men were very proud of him. I beg to offer my deepest sympathy with yourself and family"*

Frank is buried in Gommecourt British Cemetery No.2 along with over 1,350 other Commonwealth casualties. Sadly about half of these are unidentified.

He qualified for a 1915 Star, British War Medal and Victory Medal, and his father should have received a Memorial Plaque and Scroll.

There is a probate record for Frank, and he left his effects to his father.

40356 PRIVATE ERIC DAVIES
1/5th Battalion South Lancashire Regiment

ERIC WAS THE THIRD BROTHER to die and unfortunately there is not much to be told about his army career. There was nothing published in the local newspapers, and no service record has survived either.

His family believe that this is his photograph, but he is wearing a 6th Battalion King's Liverpool cap badge. If this is him then it is likely that he enlisted and trained with them in the UK (just as three of his brothers had done a couple of years earlier). Towards the end of the war it was often the case that a recruit having trained in the UK was sent out to whichever Regiment was in most urgent need of reinforcements.

An expert on the South Lancashires believes that his number (40356) was probably not issued until early 1917 and this ties in with his age.

He would only have been 19 at the end of 1916, and strictly speaking men were not supposed to be sent overseas until 19 years old. He may well have been posted to France as part of a reinforcement draft in early 1917.

At some point Eric was taken prisoner, this much is certain, and the following is a likely account of what happened next.

He was probably wounded when he was taken prisoner, and it is known that a German army hospital was situated in Conde-sur-L'Escaut at that time, adjacent to what is now the cemetery. Eric would have been taken there where he died of his wounds on 3rd April 1918 aged just 20. He was buried very close to the hospital which was believed to be on the newer part of the cemetery (on the left of the photograph).

Conde-sur-l'Escaut Communal Cemetery, is north of Valenciennes near the Belgian border.

The cemetery contains 99 Commonwealth servicemen from the Great War, and 90 of these died in German hands. Eric and 86 other men are buried in one long row, as shown on the photograph

Eric qualified for the British War Medal and the Victory Medal, and his father should have received a Memorial Plaque and Scroll.

2ND LIEUTENANT ARTHUR DAVIES
Royal Garrison Artillery

ARTHUR WAS THE LAST OF the four brothers to die, and just like his brother Eric there is not much that can be told about his army career.

There was absolutely nothing in the local newspapers, his service record is not available, and his death certificate could not be provided by the General Register Office.

All that can be certain is that Arthur served in India with the Royal Garrison Artillery. His promotion to Temporary 2nd Lieutenant was listed in the London Gazette on 6th May 1918.

He died on 19th October 1918 aged 31, at Station Hospital, Rawalpindi, India (now Pakistan) and the cause of death is not known but was most likely illness, given that it was peacetime in India.

His probate record adds that he was attached to 2nd Brigade Mountain Artillery and left effects of £228 to his father William.

13

However, the Royal Artillery Museum have offered the information that a different Mountain Battery R.G.A. (9th Brigade) had suffered losses in an Influenza outbreak in Rawalpindi in October. Four Officers and one wife had died.

It looks almost certain that Arthur died of what was later called Spanish Flu, which killed millions of people all over the world in 1918 & 1919.

A photograph of his headstone in Rawalpindi is shown below.

Rawalpindi War Cemetery contains 257 burials from the First World War period and 101 from the Second World War.

Because Arthur did not serve in a "theatre of war" he only qualified for a British War Medal. His father should have received a Memorial Plaque and Scroll.

He is also commemorated simply as "A. Davies" on the memorial at the Liverpool Cotton Exchange, Old Hall Street (his place of work).

24159 PRIVATE AARON WHITE MM
11ᵗʰ + 15ᵗʰ Battalion Cheshire Regiment

AARON WAS BORN IN BEBINGTON (or New Ferry) towards the end of 1877 or January 1878.

His parents were Joseph White from Liverpool, a Platelayer on the Railways, and Harriet (nee Molyneux) from Bebington. In 1881 they were living at No.13 Alma Cottages, New Ferry with seven of their eight children.

By 1891 they were at No.13 Leatham Road, New Ferry. Aaron was 13 now but still at school. The eight children in birth order were Margaret Anne, Joseph, Thomas, Nellie, James, John Molyneux, Aaron, and William.

In 1896 Harriet died at the age of just 55 and so the family were soon to split up. Sadly it also looks likely that the youngest child William died the year after his mother.

On the 1901 census Aaron and his father were living at 44 Oakleigh Grove with Aaron's sister Nellie, (Nellie had married Thomas Cooper at St.Andrews in 1895). Aaron was now working as a Labourer in a Brickworks, probably in New Ferry, but he joined Lever Brothers in 1903 and was still working there when the war intervened.

On 19th October 1907 Aaron married Mary Robinson at St. Mary & St. Helen's church in Neston, Aaron's address was given as 16 Primrose Hill, Port Sunlight, very convenient for the soap works. This was actually his older brother John's house, and he was also working at Levers.

By 1911 Aaron & Mary were in their own home, at No.1 Bunns Place, New Ferry. They had been married for three years now and had a two year old daughter Mary. Aaron was working in the Tin Box department at Levers and his 76 year old father was also living with them – and he was also still working, as a Labourer for the Council! Aaron had also become a very enthusiastic gardener by this time, and he exhibited at all the local horticultural shows with great success.

It should also be mentioned here that the couple went on to have more children, it is believed that there were five altogether, Mary, Robert, Daniel, Aaron, and Joseph.

Despite being 36 years old when war was declared Aaron soon volunteered and it is believed that he enlisted at the end of 1914. No service record has survived but after studying his medal index card it is believed that he attested to the 11th Battalion Cheshire Regiment at first. At the time of his death the Lever Brothers magazine *"Progress"* reported that he had been in the army since 31st December 1914, so this is presumably the date that he enlisted.

Aaron would have trained at Bournemouth initially, but the Battalion moved to Aldershot in May 1915 until they were posted to France, arriving there on 25th September 1915.

The 9th, 10th & 11th Battalions of the Cheshires were all in the 75th Brigade of the 25th Division.

In July 1916 they took part in the Battle of Albert, one of the preliminary actions on the Somme, and on 3rd July the 75th Brigade were reported to be in a position just east of Albert. *The Long, Long Trail* website summarises the events of this day as :

"On 3 July, 75th Brigade made a virtually unsupported and inevitably costly and unsuccessful attack in one of the awful, piecemeal, efforts to hold on to the minor gains made in the Thiepval area on 1 July."

The 11th Battalion suffered very badly, having 84 men killed in action on this dreadful day, Roland Green from Bromborough Pool was one of them, and his story is told elsewhere in this book. A more

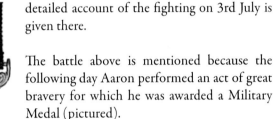

detailed account of the fighting on 3rd July is given there.

The battle above is mentioned because the following day Aaron performed an act of great bravery for which he was awarded a Military Medal (pictured).

The Brigade Chaplain was lying in the open, having been wounded. Seeing this, Aaron carried him to a place of safety while under fire from bullets and shells. Aaron himself was wounded in the left knee whilst performing the rescue and spent six weeks in hospital recuperating.

Although Aaron had been with the 11th Battalion of the Cheshires up to now, at some point before his death in 1918 he was transferred to the 15th Battalion (Cheshire Bantams). As he most probably received the six weeks treatment for his knee injury in the UK he would not have returned to the front until about the middle of August, and Stephen McGreal's book *"Cheshire Bantams"* records that on 20th August the 15th Battalion received a reinforcement draft of 103 men from the 11th Battalion and 61 from the 10th Battalion. So it seems quite likely that Aaron was one of these.

There is little else to reveal about his service until 4th February 1918 when Aaron died of wounds at the age of 40.

There was no report of his death in the Birkenhead News, and it is not possible to be certain how or when he received his wounds. According to the Battalion war diary they were out of the line and took no casualties during the last few days of January. From the 1st February they were holding trenches near Poelcapelle, and it was a pretty quiet time, only having one man killed in the first 4 days of the month.

It does seem certain that Aaron was wounded between 1st and 3rd February because he is buried close by in Duhallow Advanced Dressing Station Cemetery, about 1 mile north of Ypres. This cemetery is just a mile or two south west of Poelcapelle, so Aaron probably died very soon after his injuries.

Duhallow contains over 1,500 Commonwealth casualties, and a photograph of Aaron's headstone is shown here. The MM denotes his Military Medal.

He is also commemorated on the Port Sunlight memorial, and apart from the MM he was awarded a 1915 Star, British War Medal, and Victory Medal.

His wife Mary would have been sent them together with a Memorial Plaque and Scroll, however by the time she received them she had got remarried to John Blakeway in 1920.

It is worth mentioning that it was the custom at Lever Brothers during the war for winners of gallantry medals to be rewarded with a gold watch.

Aaron himself was rewarded in this fashion for his bravery in winning the Military Medal. He may have been granted leave especially for the occasion, because the watch was presented to him in person towards the end of 1916 by none other than Sir William Lever. There was an article in the company magazine *"Progress"* (December issue) about the presentation and an artists impression of four of the recipients of gold watches was printed – as shown below.

Corpl. Slack (D.C.M.), Corpl. Allan (M.M.), Corpl. McInnes (Mention), and Pte. White (M.M.).

Lynne, a great niece of Aaron, has given me a nice little tale about him to finish this story :

Lynne's mother Emily was born shortly after Aaron was killed, but the last time he had leave from the army he came to see his sister-in-law and left a mysterious German coin and a nice embroidered card for the baby to be - from its uncle Aaron.

It turns out that the coin was in fact a German beer token from the city of Kiel, and the baby was a girl. Aaron had most probably picked it up on the battlefield somewhere and thought it was a real coin. Emily still cherishes the token and the embroidered card.

Aaron was also the uncle of Samuel White ("Lancaster") whose story is told later in the book.

MERSEY 4/49 ABLE SEAMAN MATTHEW FRAY
Royal Navy Volunteer Reserve

MATTHEW WAS BORN IN KEARSLEY (between Manchester & Bolton) on 13th March 1895. He was one of 3 surviving children of Lincoln Fray (a printer) and his wife Clara, the whole family were born in or around Kearsley but by 1901 they were all living at 62 Greendale Road, Port Sunlight. Matthew attended Port Sunlight day school and had an older sister Hilda and a younger brother George. The family moved to Bebington in 1899 for the good employment prospects provided by Lever Brothers. The 1911 census reveals that Lincoln was working as a Printer at Levers, Hilda was a Nursing Sister there, and Matthew (aged 16) a Fancy Cardbox Maker. They attended the Wesleyan Church in Lower Bebington.

Life was good, Lever Brothers were providing secure employment and in 1911 they had all moved just down the road to a beautiful company house at 45 Greendale Road (see photo).

MATTHEW OBVIOUSLY WANTED A BIT more adventure, and in July 1911 he left Port Sunlight to go to sea with Alfred Holt (Blue Funnel) lines, and he was at sea for two years.

So it was natural that on the outbreak of war he immediately signed up with the Nelson Battalion of the Royal Naval Division on 11th August 1914. The RND was formed in 1914 from the surplus of sailors that were not required for the Navy. He fought as a soldier at the Siege of Antwerp in October 1914, spending 3 days and 2 nights in the trenches defending the city against the German advance before having to join the retreat. Apparently the RND marched 32 miles with only one 30 minute rest before arriving at Ostend, and then on to the UK soon after.

Whilst at home it was reported in *"Progress"* (the Lever Brothers quarterly magazine) that he had great pity for the plight of the Belgian people he had seen in Antwerp and was quoted as saying: *"if the young men of England could see the poor Belgian women & children, we should soon have a great army to fight the Germans".*

On 12th December 1914 he joined *"H.M.S. Viknor"* and sailed from Jarrow on the 27th. She had previously been a Blue Star vessel named the *"Viking"* but had been commandeered by the navy and converted into an armed merchant cruiser with the purpose of patrolling the waters between Scotland and Iceland. The photo shown of her here is pre-war.

On 13th January 1915 she was near Tory island off the north west coast of Ireland and had been in wireless contact with the shore at 4pm. There was a violent storm at the time and it was also thought that the Germans had mined the area, or perhaps she was torpedoed, but whatever the reason the *Viknor* sank very quickly without even sending out a distress signal. She went down with the loss of all 291 hands, Matthew included. He was just 19.

Most of the bodies were never found and many were probably trapped on board, but over the following weeks several bodies were washed ashore along the north coast of Ireland and even places as far away as the Ayrshire coast and the Isles of Jura & Colonsay (Inner Hebrides).

Matthew's body was never officially recovered, but it is rather poignant to know that six unidentified bodies from the *Viknor* were found and buried in Rathlin (St. Thomas) churchyard on Rathmore Island (2 headstones, with 3 men in each grave) and a photo of one is shown here - epitaph "Known unto God".

There are more unidentified *Viknor* burials in Bonamargy cemetery near Ballycastle, Kilchattan churchyard on the Isle of Colonsay, Larne new cemetery, and on the Isle of Coll.

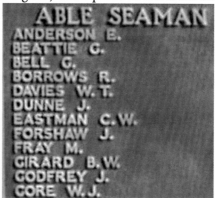

   Matthew is also commemorated on the Port Sunlight memorial, his parent's headstone in St. Andrews churchyard, the Wesleyan memorial in Lower Bebington and on the Plymouth Naval memorial (see photo).

   He was awarded the 1914 Star, British War Medal and Victory Medal. His parents would also have received a Memorial Plaque and Scroll.

   As a matter of local interest at least eight other Wirral men were lost on the *Viknor*, mostly Birkenhead men.

LIEUTENANT PERCY DALE KENDALL
10ᵗʰ Battalion Kings Liverpool Regiment

PERCY WAS BORN IN PRESCOT, Lancashire in September 1878, the son of Francis Henry and Margaret E. Kendall. Francis was a solicitor and Percy was destined to follow in his fathers footsteps. By 1891 the family were living at 284 Old Chester Road, Tranmere and the five children of the marriage were, in birth order : Francis Albert, Mary Catherine, Percy Dale, Hugh Berenger and Henry Ewing.

In 1901 they were living at 39 Highfield South in Rock Ferry and Percy was the only child at home, he was now 22 and an Articled Clerk at a solicitors office. The children were sent away for their schooling and are often missing off the censuses.

Percy was educated at Tonbridge school and then Trinity Hall, Cambridge, he was a rugby union player of some repute, being described in the local press as *"one of the greatest players of his time"*. Percy was affectionately known as *"Toggie"* to his friends and played his club rugby for Birkenhead Park, but he was also a full England international, playing several times for England and skippering the team against Scotland at Richmond in 1902. He also played 36 times for Cheshire.

Percy married Kathrine Minnie Bingham Higginson at St. Peters church, Rock Ferry on 21st April 1910 and they set up home at *"The Old Rectory"* Lower Bebington. The census summary indicates that this was No. 34 The Village, and the house may well have been sited on what is now a grassed area opposite the *"Rose & Crown"*. Percy was working as a solicitor for *"Banks, Kendall and Taylor"* in Liverpool. They had two children before the war, Janet Eulalie Bingham born 18th May 1911 and Timothy Bingham Dale born 8th October 1913.

True to his sporting instincts Percy attested to the 10th Kings Liverpool Regiment on 5th August 1914, the day after Britain had declared war on Germany! He was 3035 Private Percy Kendall for just about 10 weeks before being granted a commission on 14th October. His service record reveals that he was 5'-9½" tall, and aged 35.

The Battalion were posted overseas fairly quickly, leaving Southampton on 1st November 1914 aboard the *"S.S. Maidan"* and arriving at Le Havre later the same day.

Percy was a Lieutenant in what was popularly known as the Liverpool Scottish.

By 27th November they were occupying trenches east of Kemmel in Belgium, but were lucky enough to spend several days over Christmas out of the line in billets at Locre. They spent the whole of January in the same area.

They had been out of the line for a few days but the war diary reported that on the night of the 24th January 150 of their men took over front line trenches, with the rest of the Battalion either in support or 500 yards behind the firing line. Heavy shelling was reported on the morning of the 25th, but the diary also stated that *"the Battalian lost Lieutenant Kendall who was killed by a rifle bullet"*.

The local paper gave A little more detail from a report by a fellow officer: *". . . . poor Kendall was killed by what must have been almost a chance shot through one of the loopholes in the trench, and we buried him beside Fred Turner in the little churchyard near the firing line the same night. He was one of our best officers, and will be much missed. We had a Private, young Pollexfen, killed the same day, also a good man."*

Lieutenant Fred Turner was from Liverpool and had been killed on 10th January, he was a Scottish rugby union international. Guy Pollexfen was from Oxton, Birkenhead, and was a former head boy at Birkenhead Institute.

Very soon after Percys death, on Friday 5th February, a memorial service was held for him at St. Nicholas' church (near the Liver Buildings) in Liverpool. Remarkably the church was not only packed to the rafters but over 200 mourners were unable to get in. Lord Derby was in attendance, and part of the service was conducted by Archdeacon Ford the rector of Bebington. Little did the Archdeacon know that he would lose his own son at Ploegsteert, Belgium before the year was out. (see this story later in the book)

Percy was aged 36 and is buried in Kemmel Churchyard about 5 miles south west of Ypres, one of just 25 Commonwealth casualties from the Great War buried here. Percy's headstone has the comment "Known to be buried in this cemetery". There is a record of him being buried there, but unfortunately the burials were later disturbed by heavy shelling (long before CWGC headstones were erected.) The epitaph reads :

"Their glory shall not be blotted out"

Percy was awarded a 1914 Star, British War Medal and Victory Medal, and his wife Kathrine would have received a Memorial Plaque and Scroll.

Percy's younger brother Hugh served in the war as a Lieutenant/ Acting Captain in the Royal Field Artillery, and his brother Henry served in the Royal Navy as a Chaplain. Both won a British War Medal and Victory medal and survived the war. Henry was also awarded an OBE in later life.

As a rather sad footnote, Percy's British War Medal is known to be in a private collection. It is not known where the 1914 Star and Victory Medal are.

522 SAPPER FRANCIS JOSEPH SMITH
Cheshire Field Company – Royal Engineers

HE WAS ALWAYS REFERRED TO as Frank, on the memorial in St.Andrews and in newspaper articles at the time of his death.

Frank was born about 1890 in Seacombe, Wallasey. His father William was from Blackpool originally and was a Book Keeper, his mother Mary was from Liverpool.

In 1891 the family were living in Seacombe, and Frank was 1 year old. No official record of his birth can be found but 1891 agrees with all the census records and also the age given when he died.

By 1891 the father was working as a Book Keeper for Lever Brothers and they were living in a beautiful company house at No.1 Bath Street in Port Sunlight (see photo).

There were six children of the marriage and five of them were still alive on the 1911 census, by which time they had moved to 308 New Chester Road, Port Sunlight.

In birth order the children were : Richard A, William, Catherine Esther, Francis Joseph, Robert and Harold John.

Sadly for these children, especially young Harold who was only 8, their mother died in March 1912.

Frank was working as a Plumber in 1911, but not at Lever Brothers - although he was working for them soon afterwards.

He enlisted with the Cheshire Field Company of the Royal Engineers very soon after war was declared, and he was posted over to France on 11th December 1914. This was the original draft and it also included John Williams and Walter Smith of Higher Bebington who were to die at Hooge in June 1916.

Frank spent Christmas overseas, and with no service records available we don't know anything more until a few months later in May 1915 when he was digging trenches near Ypres and he was hit in the thigh by a bullet. His thigh was fractured and after being evacuated to Boulogne he was soon back in the UK, where he was treated at the Southern Hospital in Birmingham.

There must have been complications with his wound because he died on 18th June aged just 24.

His body was brought back to Port Sunlight and he was buried with military honours in Bebington Cemetery on Tuesday 22nd June.

The cortege passed through Port Sunlight village on the way to the cemetery, his coffin draped with a Union Jack. Four members of the Royal Engineers acted as bearers and after the Last Post was sounded three volleys were fired over the grave.

Two of his brothers were also in the army but were given leave to attend his funeral and more mention of them is given later.

Frank is buried in the same grave as his mother Mary and a photograph of the headstone in Bebington cemetery is shown here.

He qualified for a 1914-15 Star, British War Medal, and Victory Medal. His father William would have received a Memorial Plaque and Scroll.

Frank is also commemorated on the Port Sunlight memorial.

Frank had two brothers who also served in the war. Robert, who at the time of Frank's death was in training with the 17th Battalion Cheshire Regiment (the Bantams) and William who was with the Denbigh Hussars.

R/18704 LANCE CORPORAL RALPH WILLIAMS
9th Battalion - Kings Royal Rifle Corps

RALPH WAS BORN IN BEBINGTON in 1894, the first child of Albert and Rachel Williams. Albert was from Brecon originally but he had married Rachel Appleton (a Bebington girl) at St.Andrews in 1893. He was working as a Tallow & Oil Sampler at Lever Brothers in 1901 and the couple were living at No.27 Bromborough Road with four children. By 1911 they were living at No.13 Bromborough Road, Albert was still in the same job but they had added two more children and sadly lost one. Ralph and his brother Albert were now both working at Lever Brothers, Ralph as a Soap Piler.

The six children were, in birth order : Ralph, Albert, Noel, John, Ernest (died aged 5) and Florence.

He had been a member of the St.Andrew's Church Lads' Brigade and gained the rank of Staff Sergeant, so he seems to have had an aptitude for soldiering at a young age. He was also a bell ringer at St.Andrew's church.

On the outbreak of war he very quickly enlisted as 12648 Private Williams with the York and Lancaster Regiment at Liverpool on 1st September 1914. At his medical he was just over 5'-7" and 8½ stone, fresh complexion, blue eyes, brown hair. He was also C.of E.

Ralph must have been disappointed to say the least when he was discharged as "medically unfit" on 20th November, but this was at a time when the army were really selective and could afford to reject some of the new recruits.

He later enlisted with another Regiment, the King's Royal Rifle Corps, he was more successful this time and he was placed in the 9th Battalion (15th Platoon of "D" Company).

Ralph's service record has not survived and so it is not possible to determine exactly when he was posted overseas, but it was not before January 1916.

He managed a few days home leave at the end of September 1917 and returned to the front on October 2nd.

The Battalion were in Belgium at this time fighting at Passchendaele.

The war diary reported that they had had a relatively easy time of it in September, and the first couple of weeks of October also saw very few casualties. However on the 16th October they relieved the 7th Battalion Rifle Brigade in trenches opposite Polderhoek Chateau. They set off for the front line at 4.15pm and suffered an intense enemy artillery barrage on the way up. They took several casualties but were finally in position just after midnight. The heavy shelling continued all night particularly so between 5.30am – 6.30am. Notwithstanding the dreadful time they were having, the war diary contained a nice bit of trench humour on the morning of 17th. Apparently a message had arrived for the Medical Officer asking him to *"state how many ablution benches and latrine buckets are needed for the Battalion"* and the following reply was sent back *"The men are using shell holes for both purposes, no additional ones required".*

The night of the 17th passed quietly.

It is almost certain that it was on the evening of the 16th or in the early hours and morning of the 17th that Ralph sustained serious injuries to his right thigh and leg, left hand, and face. He was treated at 2nd Canadian Casualty Clearing Station on 18th October and the Chaplain there, Robert Howe, wrote to Ralph's parents warning them that he was very seriously wounded. The following day he had to write another letter telling them that Ralph had passed away at 11.45pm the previous evening. He was 24 years old.

Ralph was buried nearby in Lijssenthoek Military Cemetery, about 8 miles west of Ypres. This is a big cemetery with almost 10,000 Commonwealth burials from the Great War. A photo of Ralph's headstone is shown on the following page.

The epitaph chosen by his parents reads :

"For Country Liberty and Truth
He gave his Youth"

Ralph qualified for a British War Medal and Victory Medal, and his parents would have received a Memorial Plaque and Scroll.

He is also commemorated on the Port Sunlight memorial.

After his death there were many tributes to Ralph in the *"Birkenhead News"* including one from : *his devoted fiancée Nellie and all at No.6 The Village.*

The Church Lads' Brigade occasionally held dances, and one had been scheduled for 27th October 1917. A letter was circulated at short notice cancelling the event out of respect for Ralph. The dance was held the week after on 3rd November and it is sure to have been a more sombre event than usual.

All four of the Williams sons served in the war and fortunately the other three survived.

W/961 Pte. Albert Williams served with the 13th Cheshires from the start of the war and was seriously wounded at the Somme in 1916, receiving shrapnel wounds to his neck and left shoulder. He was discharged from the army on 30th September 1916 and received a Silver War Badge. He returned to work in the Timber Stores at Lever Brothers even though he had lost the use of his left arm.

61682 Pte. Noel Williams enlisted with the 3rd Cheshires but probably didn't serve overseas.

John Williams also enlisted but because of his age he probably didn't go overseas either.

R/37033 RIFLEMAN FREDERICK HARDWICK
16th Battalion – King's Royal Rifle Corps

FREDERICK WAS BORN IN BEBINGTON in 1887. His mother was 22 year old Sarah Hardwick and Frederick was born out of wedlock. Sarah was working as a Servant for the Feilden family at Bebington Hall on the 1881 & 1891 censuses and Frederick was being brought up by Sarah's parents, the wonderfully named Enos Nimrod Hardwick and his wife Martha. They lived at No.9 The Village.

Frederick's grandmother died in 1894, but happily by 1901 the rest of the family were reunited. Enos, daughter Martha, Sarah and Frederick were all living at 5 Church Road.

In 1911 Enos, Sarah and Frederick were still at 5 Church Road and Enos, now aged 80, was working as a Warehouse Porter at a Borax manufacturer (possibly Lever Brothers). Frederick was 23 now and employed as a Jobbing Gardener.

There was nothing in the local newspapers regarding Frederick's war service, and his service papers were destroyed in the 1940 London Blitz so it cannot be certain when he joined the army. However his medal card confirms that he didn't get posted overseas until 1916 at the earliest.

What is certain though is that he married Bessie Britland at St. James' church in Christleton near Chester in the last quarter of 1917. Unless he was on leave from the army at the time, it seems likely that Frederick went to France early in 1918.

He had joined the 16th Battalion of the King's Royal Rifle Corps at Chester, and trained in the UK as No.TR/13/268381/2.

In March 1918 the Battalion were in the Zonnebeke area, north east of Ypres.

Frederick died of wounds on 21st March and it is not possible to be sure just when he received these wounds. The Battalion war diary reported that they were out of the line on the 18th, but moved to a support line in the evening and took no casualties.

On the 19th they were still in support but suffered heavy shelling with gas and high explosives. Two other ranks were killed and there were several gas casualties.

On the 20th (still in support) they were shelled with gas in the morning and suffered several casualties. The rest of the day was much quieter.

It is very likely that Frederick was wounded by shelling or gas on the 19th or 20th. He was taken to 99th Field Ambulance and died on the 21st March 1918 at the age of 30.

Frederick is buried close by in Potijze Chateau Grounds Cemetery and a photograph of his headstone is shown here.

He qualified for a British War Medal and Victory Medal, and his widow Bessie would also have received a Memorial Plaque and Scroll.

After the war Bessie was using an address in Chorlton-cum-Hardy.

HARDWICK Frederick of 5 Church-road Lower Bebington Cheshire a private in the King's Royal Rifle Corps died 21 March 1918 at the 99th Field Ambulance in France Probate Chester 22 August to Bessie Hardwick widow. Effects £212 3s. 7d.

22003 CORPORAL WILLIAM HERBERT SUCKLEY
17th Battalion – Cheshire Regiment

HERBERT AS HE PREFERRED TO be known, was the third of eight or nine children born to his parents John Herbert & Mary Jane Suckley, both originally from the Wrexham area of North Wales. They soon moved to the Wirral after their marriage in 1891, and young Herbert was born in Bebington in early 1897. His siblings in birth order were Mary Elizabeth, David John, (Herbert), Oliver Charles, Catherine Esther, Moses Henry, James Harold and George Osborne.

After leaving school Herbert worked as a lamp cleaner at the Provincial Motor Company for a while before joining Lever Brothers and working in the No.2 Soapery (Frame Room), his father was also employed there as a Motor Driver. Herbert was a member of the Boys Brigade for over two years.

He enlisted with the Cheshire Bantams, possibly in August 1915, these were battalions originally formed to take men smaller than the usual minimum height of 5'-3" and he was training with the 17th Reserve Battalion right through 1916. He was obviously doing very well too, having been promoted to Lance Corporal rather quickly and then later to Corporal.

On 9th January 1917 the Battalion were in training at Prees Heath camp near Whitchurch, and the *"Birkenhead News"* reported that Herbert (still only 20 years old) was instructing some men on the use of high explosive bombs (nowadays called hand grenades).

There was an explosion and Herbert was mortally wounded. Corporal Crew made a gallant attempt to resuscitate him but was himself rendered unconscious by fumes, fortunately Corporal Crew made a full recovery and was able to attend Herbert's funeral.

His parents received a letter of sympathy from the Captain & Adjutant of the battalion, and Lt. May who was in charge of the instruction class wrote :

"He has worked with me for the past year, which perhaps makes me feel his loss more deeply than anyone else in the Battalion, as we were always the best of pals right from the first. During the time he was on my staff as bombing instructor he gave me every satisfaction, and was always a splendid soldier. Both officers and men thought a great deal of him, and

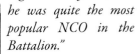

he was quite the most popular NCO in the Battalion."

The funeral at St. Andrew's church took place with full military honours on Saturday 13th January, the cortege leaving his parents home at 60

Bromborough Road, Lower Bebington for the very short journey to the church.

HERBERT'S OLDER BROTHER DAVID HAD enlisted with the Cheshires on 9th January 1915 but was discharged a few days later with a serious heart problem. David died in 1918 aged 24 and is buried in the same grave as Herbert, it seems reasonable to assume that his heart problems caught up with him. Both brothers are commemorated on the Port Sunlight memorial.

Their younger brother Oliver (born 1899) also joined up with the South Lancashires before the end of the war and was awarded the British War Medal and Victory Medal.

Herbert himself did not qualify for any war medals because he did not serve overseas, but his parents would have received a Memorial Plaque and Scroll.

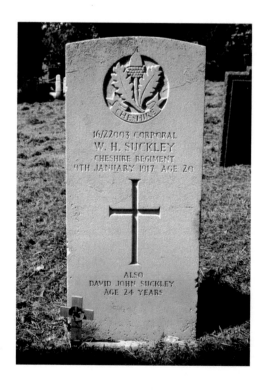

MAJOR RICHARD LE BRUN NICHOLSON
MC+BAR
11ᵗʰ Battalion Cheshire Regiment (attached to 1/6ᵗʰ Battalion)

RICHARD WAS BORN IN BEBINGTON on 8th August 1895. He was the only son of William Richard and Ethel Le Brun Nicholson. William was born in Rock Ferry and he became a very successful businessman. He was the son of a Provision Merchant and was sent away to boarding school in Birkdale, Southport and his expensive education paid off.

He married Ethel in 1891, there is no record of the marriage here but Ethel was born in Ontario, Canada and they may have married there. The 1891 census reveals that William, aged just 26, was already a Ship Owner, and they were living on their own in Rock Ferry but employing a servant.

41

THEY WENT ON TO HAVE three children, Freda Marion in 1892 , Richard Le Brun, and Lois Scarth in 1896.

In 1901 they were living at No.31 Church Road, Lower Bebington. This address no longer exists but ironically it is likely to have been on the site of the present day No.29, and right next door to where the War Memorial was to be built 22 years later. They had their three children with them now and they were employing a Governess and two servants.

Richard was educated at the Leas school in Hoylake at first, but from the age of 14 he attended Loretto school in Musselburgh near Edinburgh. He was a Sergeant in the Officer Training Corps there. Richard finished his education in 1914 and took up employment as a Shipping Apprentice. This was very short term of course, because once war was declared Richard volunteered almost immediately.

His service record reveals that he went to Seaforth on 19th August 1914 to enlist with the Kings Liverpool Regiment, but for one reason or another he didn't pursue that option. He then travelled down to 24 St. James' Street in London on 7th September and joined the 16th Battalion Middlesex Regiment as 187 Pte. Richard Nicholson. They were a Public Schools Battalion so perhaps he felt more comfortable with them.

His army medical records his height as 5'-6½" and weight as 9st 9lbs. He had an appendix scar, and was of light complexion, with green eyes and light hair. He was also Church of England. The family address was now given as Nelson's Croft, Bebington and although this is now a built up road there is one grand house which seems likely to have been the one the Nicholsons had moved to (see photo).

His career in the Middlesex Regiment proved extremely short lived because later the same month he was offered a commission in the 11th Battalion of the Cheshires which he took up. He was now 2nd Lieutenant Richard Nicholson, and he carried on his training with the Cheshires, first at Bournemouth and then Aldershot. During this training period, in July 1915, he was promoted to Captain. The Battalion was posted overseas on 26th September 1915 and arrived in France probably the same day.

In July 1916 the 11th Cheshires were at the Somme and involved in the attack on Thiepval. On 3rd July they were ordered to attack the Leipzig Salient, a German strongpoint which had been holding up the advance. They went over the top at 6.20am as planned but the attack went disastrously wrong. They advanced over no mans land in perfect order but 50 yards from the German trenches they were met by heavy machine gun fire. The Battalion war diary noted that *"Line after line of troops were mown down."* What was left of the Battalion withdrew back to their jumping off point. Of the 677 Officers and men who had gone into action only 356 were able to answer roll call the next morning.

5 Officers and 84 men had been killed and the rest were missing or wounded.

Roland Green from Bromborough Pool was one of those killed and his is the next story to be told in this book.

Richard Nicholson suffered a gunshot wound to his left forearm on this day, the bullet luckily having gone straight through without breaking any bones. On 5th he embarked on board *"H.M.T. Egypt"* at Le Havre and arrived at Southampton later the same day. He was treated for his injuries at the 1st London General Hospital for several weeks before returning to duty, at first with the 50th Training Reserve Battalion at Prees Heath, Whitchurch on 4th September.

In June 1917 the 11th Battalion were to play a part in the Battle of Messines in Belgium, and Richard was awarded a Military Cross this month. It was most likely won on the first day of the battle on 7th June, when the Battalion went over the top at 6.50am.

The citation for his M.C. reads: *"For conspicuous gallantry and devotion to duty. He led his company with great skill and dash to its objective, although under hostile fire from a flank. His company captured many prisoners."*

The attack was deemed a complete success, although 1 officer and 25 men had been killed.

Richard was still a Captain, but he showed great courage once again nine months later when he was awarded a Bar to his Military Cross. This was probably won at the Battle of the Lys during the period of the German Spring Offensive in March and April 1918.

This time the citation read : *"For conspicuous gallantry and devotion to duty. When his company was holding a sunken road, the enemy penetrated their left flank. He immediately organised a defensive flank, and held on to his position for several hours against repeated attacks accompanied by very heavy machine gun fire, until ordered to withdraw. He withdrew his company intact under cover of his Lewis gunners, with very few casualties. He showed powers of command of a high order."*

On 17th June 1918 the 11th Battalion were reduced to cadre strength as part of a re-organisation, and most of the men were transferred to the 6th Battalion. Richard was one of them, and about this time he was also promoted to acting Major, perhaps before he was transferred. The promotion was no doubt a result of his actions in April.

By August 1918 a victory for the Allies looked certain, but there was still much fighting to be done. Richard was with the 6th Battalion of the Cheshires and towards the end of the month they were near Locre, about 6 miles south west of Ypres. The Battalion war diary reported that at dusk on 27th they had moved into front line trenches south east of Locre and they were still there on the 30th. During this quiet time they had only lost one officer killed. At 4.30 pm on 30th August they received a report that the enemy were withdrawing and patrols were immediately sent out to ascertain the situation. By midnight the whole Battalion had advanced with practically no opposition.

The advance continued through pouring rain during the early hours of the 31st and by 8am they had passed through Dranoutre. Shortly after this they met with strong enemy resistance from machine gun and artillery fire, the Germans were holding a system of trenches on top of a ridge. They could not proceed any further and were relieved by the 7th Royal Irish Regiment at dusk.

The war diary reported light casualties in spite of heavy shelling throughout the latter part of the day - 1 Officer and 4 Other Ranks killed and 16 wounded.

Richard was the Officer killed, having just turned 23 years of age. One report indicated that he had been killed by a shell.

He is buried in Godewaersvelde British Cemetery about 10 miles west of Ypres and a photograph of his headstone is shown on the following page. This cemetery contains almost 1,000 Commonwealth casualties of the Great War.

The epitaph chosen by his parents reads :

"Gloria in Excelsis Deo"

Apart from his two Military Crosses he also qualified for a 1915 Star, British War Medal, and Victory Medal. His parents would also have received a Memorial Plaque and Scroll.

12683 LANCE CORPORAL ROLAND GREEN
11ᵗʰ Battalion Cheshire Regiment

ROLAND WAS THE YOUNGEST CHILD of George and Elizabeth Anne Green, he was born in Bromborough in 1897. His father was an Engineering Fitter from Battersea originally and his mother from Devon, but they appear to have married in Birkenhead in 1885. Roland's older brother & sister were George Herbert and Ethel.

On the 1911 census the father George was working as an Engineer in Prices Candle Works, and young Roland having left the Bromborough Pool school was working as an assistant in a local Co-op shop aged 14.

He was a Sergeant in the Bebington Church Lads Brigade, and he may have commenced work in Prices before the war started.

THE FAMILY HAD LIVED AT No. 37 South View in Bromborough Pool for many years although Roland was the only child at home by 1911. He would have known Harry George who lived just 4 doors away and his story is told elsewhere in this book.

Roland's sister Ethel married Robert Littler towards the end of 1910 at St. Barnabas's church in Bromborough, and he will be mentioned again later.

Roland enlisted with the Cheshires at Birkenhead on 1st September 1914, under age at just 17, but his service record reveals that he gave his year of birth as 1894 in order to be accepted. Nevertheless he was a mature 17, standing 5'-9" tall, 10½ stone, with blue eyes, brown hair and a fresh complexion.

He was posted to the 8th Battalion at first and trained at Chiseldon and Pirbright. Whilst training in Purbright he overstayed his pass by 2 days and received 3 days confined to barracks with loss of pay as a punishment.

The Battalion was posted overseas on 26th June 1915. The final destination was to be Gallipoli but they disembarked in Egypt on the way.

They landed at Suvla Bay in the heat of the Summer and on 13th August Roland reported to the 13th casualty clearing station with dysentery. This was a common occurrence in Gallipoli, but Roland had it very serious and was invalided home to England. He was admitted to a clearing hospital in Eastleigh on 15th September, and after recuperating he was reported to be training at Leasowe the following month. He remained in the UK until 28th March 1916.

He was finally posted overseas again, this time to France as a Lance Corporal with the 11th Battalion. He must have arrived with his unit in early April 1916, just in time for the Somme.

July 1st was the infamous first day of the Battle of the Somme, with about 19,000 Commonwealth men killed. The 11th Cheshires were not directly involved on the 1st but were thrown into the attack on the 3rd.

They were ordered to be part of an attack on the Leipzig Salient, south of Thiepval, and at 6.20 am they went over the top accompanied by the 8th Border Regiment.

The war diary reported that they crossed no mans land in perfect order but 50 yards short of the German barbed wire heavy machine gun fire brought them to a halt. They were simply mown down, and with most of their officers out of action the Adjutant, Captain Hill, made the decision that those still on their feet should get back to their jumping off point.

The Regimental History records that on the following morning *"no organised body of men existed"*. Of the 20 officers and 657 other ranks who went over the top at 6.20am only 6 officers and 350 men came out of the trenches on the 4th July.

Roland (aged just 20) was one of the men killed, about 89 in total on the day although more would die of their wounds in the following days.

A soldier friend of his wrote to his parents : *"His death was almost instantaneous, as we were ordered to attack at a certain time. He was one of the first over the parapet but he fell back in the open wounded, only to rise and cheer us on. But sad to say he was shot again and fell as a soldier and a man."*

Roland is buried in Lonsdale Cemetery, Authuille, and a photo of his headstone is shown here. There are over 1,500 Commonwealth casualties in this cemetery and sadly about half of them are unidentified.

He qualified for a 1915 Star, British War Medal and Victory Medal, his parents would also have received a Memorial Plaque and Scroll. Roland is also commemorated on the Bromborough Pool memorial (inside & outside St. Matthew's church).

Going back to his brother-in-law Robert Littler, mentioned at the start of this story. After marrying Roland's sister Ethel the couple were living with her parents in 1914.

Robert was working in the time & wages department at Lever Brothers but also joined up at the start of the war, with the 9th Cheshires.

He was eventually promoted to Company Quartermaster Sergeant and was awarded a Meritorious Service Medal.

CH/1132(S) CORPORAL HERBERT WILSON
Royal Marines Light Infantry

HERBERT WAS BORN IN GORTON, Manchester on Christmas Day 1896. He was the son of Henry and Martha Alice Wilson (nee Purchess). Henry was born in Haddenham, Buckinghamshire originally but he had married Martha (from Manchester) at Chorlton-cum-Hardy in 1892. On the 1901 census he was living in Bread Street, Gorton and working as a Machine Driller. The couple eventually had ten children (in birth order) Thomas Henry, Wilfred, Herbert, Joseph, Rhoda, John, Alice, Samuel, Ruth and May.

In about 1907 they moved to Storeton, living at "Quarry Cottage" and seven of the children were still at home on the 1911 census. Herbert was now 14 and working as an Errand Boy for a Contractor, his father was a Labourer for a Building Contractor (no doubt the same one that Herbert was working for).

At some point between 1911 and 1917 they moved again, this time to "Smithy Cottage" Spital, Bebington. There was certainly a Henry Wilson working there as a Blacksmith by 1917 and it can be safely assumed that it was Herbert's father because memorial archive papers from the early 1920's give Herbert's next of kin as "Mr.& Mrs. Wilson at Smithy Cottage, Spital."

Luckily Herbert has service papers which reveal that he enlisted as CH/1132(S) Private Herbert Wilson with the Royal Marine Light Infantry in Liverpool on 1st November 1915, just before his 19th birthday. The CH prefix was for the Chatham R.M.L.I. Division, in Kent.

His medical recorded his height as 5'-6 with fresh complexion, grey eyes, and brown hair. His religion was Wesleyan. He also listed his trade as "Soap Maker" and so we can be pretty sure that he was working for Lever Brothers in Port Sunlight before enlisting.

He was immediately posted to the Royal Marine recruitment depot in Deal, but he was soon transferred to the Chatham Depot Barracks for training.

On 29th May 1916 he was posted for service with the Royal Marine Brigade at their base camp at Blandford in Dorset.

He was posted overseas on 3rd September 1916 as part of a draft to the Royal Naval Division's 190th Brigade Machine Gun Company, arriving at Le Havre on 5th September.

On 13th November he received gunshot wounds to his right forearm, right shoulder, and left thigh and he was invalided back to the UK a few days later.

It is probable that he sustained these injuries during the attack by the Royal Naval Division at the Ancre.

After a period of recuperation Herbert returned to Blandford, and was promoted to Lance Corporal on 21st March 1917. Shortly after this he attended an Infantry course at Tidworth between 30th May and 21st July. During this period, on 25th June, he was again promoted - this time to Corporal, and he qualified for a good conduct badge on 31st October after two years service. A physical training course followed in late November/early December 1917.

Presumably Herbert was now well recovered from his injuries, and he was posted overseas again on 23rd July 1918 as part of a reinforcement draft. He embarked at Folkestone and arrived at Boulogne the same day. From Boulogne he travelled to the Base Depot in Calais. On 1st September 1918 about 100 Royal Marines, including Herbert, were detached to Anson Battalion of the Royal Naval Division.

They were destined to play a part in the Battle of the Canal-du-Norde from 27th September to 1st October.

On September 27th the Battalion war diary reported that just after midnight they moved off from Queant (between Arras and Cambrai) to a concentration area west of Moeuvres.

At zero hour (time not given) they crossed the Canal-du-Norde. Opposition was met along the Hindenburg system & they had to move up through this area in going forward. The Royal Marines were on the left (with the Royal Irish in support) and the 190th Brigade on the right. The advance continued but when crossing a ridge they encountered heavy machine gun fire. With artillery support the advance again continued, eventually capturing Graincourt. They took up a position in the *"Brown Line"* and an enemy counter attack was driven off.

It is very likely that Henry was mortally wounded on this day. He suffered shell wounds (shrapnel) to his back and right leg and was treated for his injuries by the 149th Royal Naval Field Ambulance, but died on the 29th September aged just 21.

Herbert is buried in Hermies Hill British Cemetery, one of over 1,000 Commonwealth casualties buried here. A photograph of his headstone is shown.

Herbert qualified for a British War Medal and Victory Medal and these were issued to his mother in the early 1920's. She would have also received a Memorial Plaque and Scroll.

He is also commemorated on the Port Sunlight memorial.

031601 PRIVATE ERNEST GEORGE LEATHER
Cheshire Regiment and Army Ordnance Corps

ERNEST WAS BORN IN WARRINGTON in the last quarter of 1879, and it appears that his father Thomas died in 1884 and maybe his mother soon after. He is difficult to trace after that until 1911, but in 1901 there was a George Leather aged 20 living with William and Martha Greenall in Leigh (Martha's maiden name was Leather and she was looking after stepson George and his sister Isabella) – it could possibly be him.

Sometime after his schooling our Ernest Leather took up a 7 year apprenticeship as a Cooper, and on 2nd September 1905 he married Harriet Heald at the Emmanuel church in Bold Street Warrington. By 1911 they were living at 17 Monks Street with two daughters Lucy Eileen & Marjorie A.

Ernest was now working at a "Soap Manufacturers" in the Traffic department, and of course this must have been Lever Brothers.

At some point after 1911 they moved to Lower Bebington living at 11 Ashbrook Terrace until the time of Ernest's death (see photo).

His pension record has survived although it is unreadable in places, however it does reveal that Ernest was Church of England, 5'-6" tall, 9st 8lbs, grey eyes and brown hair with a fresh complexion.

On 3rd September 1914 he enlisted as W/310 with the local 13th Battalion of the Cheshire Regiment (Wirral Pals) but was very soon deemed to be unfit for overseas service. This resulted in him being transferred to the 3rd (Reserve) Battalion in August 1915 before he was finally posted overseas to Gibraltar with the 1st Garrison Battalion of the Cheshires on 11th June 1916.

At some point in 1917 he was transferred again, this time to the Army Ordnance Corps. This may have been in connection with the downturn in his health, which was first recorded in his pension records in June 1917 while serving in Gibraltar. By the end of the year he was being treated at a hospital in Gibraltar and was eventually diagnosed as suffering with tuberculosis of the lung and left Gibraltar for England on 14th September 1918.

After arriving back in the UK he was discharged from the army on 2nd October. On 15th October he was admitted to Groesynydd Isolation Hospital, Llangelynnin, near Conway, and died there a week later on 22nd October 1918 aged 39. The cause of death was given as Phthisis Pulmonalis (TB) & influenza/pneumonia.

Ernest had been granted A Silver War Badge and his pension record confirmed that his illness was due to his war service, so his wife Harriet should have received a pension.

Ernest is commemorated on the Port Sunlight memorial and received the British War Medal for his service in Gibraltar, Harriet would probably have also received a Memorial Plaque and Scroll.

It has been impossible to locate his burial place. Conwy Archives have done a thorough search of their records and found nothing and there is no burial recorded in Bebington cemetery or St. Andrews. It is also worth noting that he should be recorded on Commonwealth War Graves because his death was attributable to his war service, this has been pointed out to them and hopefully his name will eventually be added to their records.

THE DILLON BROTHERS, ANDREW, ARTHUR AND HERBERT

THE PARENTS, JAMES AND Mary Elizabeth Dillon were both born and married in Liverpool. By 1891 though, they had moved to No.15 Bromborough Road, Lower Bebington and James was working as a Warehouseman. He also served as a member of the Lower Bebington District Council for a time. They were to have at least nine or ten children, all born in Bebington, and as far as can be certain the children, in birth order were : Margaret Ann, John, William Gavin, James, Martha Amy, Andrew, Samuel, Arthur and Herbert. Sadly, it seems that Mary died in Liverpool in 1894 aged just 37, possibly in childbirth.

In 1901 the father and children seemed to have moved next door to No.17, and by 1911 they were at No.24 (they seemed to like Bromborough Road).

In 1911 Arthur and Herbert were still living with their widowed father and the oldest child Margaret was now married and also living there with her husband and four children. Andrew (understandably) had moved out and was living as a boarder with the Guntrips at 14 Manor Place, Bromborough Pool. This was also perfect for his job at Prices Candleworks.

Three of the sons joined the army, Andrew, Herbert and Arthur - and their details before the war are given here :

Andrew was born in the first quarter of 1887, and he was working as an Errand Boy in 1901 but as mentioned previously he had a steady job at Prices Candles by 1911. He was a member of the Bebington Lodge of the RAOB, and married Florence Gore at St. Mark's in New Ferry about September 1915, very shortly before going to France with the 13th Cheshires. His army career follows separately.

Herbert was born about July 1892 and at the age of eighteen he was working locally as a Gardener. He did 2 years service in the Territorials in England before the war. Herbert had bigger plans though, and immigrated to Australia sometime between 1911 and 1914. When war was declared he lost little time in volunteering for the 1st Battalion Australian Infantry on 25th August 1914 at Randwick in Sydney.

His army career continues on the next few pages.

Finally, another brother Arthur also served in the war and he survived, but not without mishap. Because of the family connection a photograph and a few brief details of Arthur's army career are listed here.

Arthur was born very early in 1891, and by 1911 he was working as a Labourer at Lever Brothers (later working in the Dry Soap Room). He played for the Church Lads Brigade football team.

Arthur enlisted as W/896 with the 13th Battalion Cheshires on Saturday 5th September 1914 and, remarkably, he married Jenny Partington at St. Andrews church the very same day. Jenny worked at Lever Brothers, also in the Dry Soap Room, so I think we can be sure how they met!

Arthur did the same training as his older brother Andrew, and he was posted to France on 25th September 1915.

He received gun shot wounds to his left hand near Arras on 28th April 1916 and he was sent back to York hospital for treatment and recuperation. It was a very bad injury, and he was eventually discharged from the army on 20th September 1917 and awarded a Silver War Badge.

He received his injury the same day that Arthur Margerison was fatally wounded (see this story elsewhere in the book).

Apart from the Silver War Badge, Arthur qualified for a 1915 Star, British War Medal and Victory Medal.

821 PRIVATE HERBERT DILLON
1st Battalion Australian Infantry

AS MENTIONED IN THE FAMILY details, Herbert had immigrated to Australia and joined the Australian Infantry.

He has a large service record and so it has been possible to find out quite a lot about his army service.

He was 22 years old at enlistment and still employed as a Labourer. He gave his next of kin as his married sister Martha Harvey of Beaconsfield Road, New Ferry, and yet in his army will he named Miss J.M. Pugh of No.1 Victoria Place, New Ferry as sole beneficiary. Perhaps she was a girlfriend, because he didn't have a sister with the initial of "J".

His medical revealed that he was 5'-5" tall, 10½ stone with blue eyes and fair hair. He was also C.of E.

Herbert embarked at Sydney on 18th October 1914 on board an Australian transport ship, arriving in Egypt to continue their training near Cairo about the turn of the year. Although they didn't yet know it the Australians were destined to take part in the Gallipoli campaign which started on 25th April 1915, so they had a few months in Egypt to prepare for what was to come.

One of Herbert's happiest memories of army life must have been when the attached photograph was taken. It appeared in the *"Birkenhead News"* in May 1916, soon after the death of his brother Andrew and shows him riding a camel with a sphinx and a pyramid in the background.

Unfortunately it is the only photograph of Herbert that could be found.

On 1st April 1915 they received orders to prepare themselves for an amphibious assault at Gallipoli, and they left Alexandria on 10th April. After spending a further twelve days on the Greek island of Lemnos training and practicing disembarking they finally landed at Anzac Cove on the 25th April. Surprisingly the war diary reported *"no casualties"*.

The Australians managed to establish a foothold on the steep slopes above the beach, but after a terrible first day in action he very soon received a gunshot wound to his left arm and a sprained ankle. He was admitted to No.15 General Hospital on the 30th, the wound was described as only slight but he was nevertheless sent to a convalescent camp in Mustapha, Egypt. He arrived back at Gallipoli on board the *"S.S. Novian"* on 21st May, but not rejoining his Battalion until 31st May.

At 1.55am on 5th June an order was received for 100 men to advance on a position called German Officers trench in order to take out a troublesome enemy machine gun and do as much damage to the trench as possible. By 2.50am the attack took place with great success but casualties of 5 killed and 28 wounded were taken.

The diary reported nothing of any consequence for the following 2 days, yet Herbert Dillon is recorded as being killed on 7th June, aged just 22.

If he had died of wounds then it could have happened during the action on 5th June, but the official papers say *"killed in action"* so it must have been just an isolated occurrence, perhaps a shell or a sniper got him.

Herbert qualified for a 1915 Star, British War Medal and Victory

Medal and a Memorial Plaque and Scroll was posted to his sister Martha Harvey.

He is buried in Shrapnel Valley Cemetery on Gallipoli.

There are 683 Commonwealth casualties from the campaign buried here. The ground is so sandy that small box type memorials are used instead of standard headstones and a photograph of Herbert's is shown here.

W/343 PRIVATE ANDREW DILLON
13th Battalion Cheshire Regiment

ANDREW'S FAMILY DETAILS ARE GIVEN in the previous pages, along with his brothers Herbert and Arthur.

On the outbreak of war Andrew lost no time in enlisting with the 13th Battalion of the Cheshires, probably between 1st – 5th September 1914.

While he was away training the family had received the terrible news of the death of Andrew's brother Herbert at Gallipoli in June 1915.

After finishing training in Bournemouth and Aldershot, the Battalion was posted to France, arriving there on 25th September 1915. Andrew had married his girlfriend Florrie Gore just a few days or weeks before going.

Along with the other Wirral Pals, Andrew had gone through a bad time at the end of April 1916. His friends Arthur Margerison and

63

William Forsey had been killed, and his brother Arthur had received a bad injury in the same action and was back home in the UK for recuperation.

It was to get a lot worse for Andrew the following month. The war diary reported that they were still in the Zouave valley 8 miles north of Arras, and they took over front line trenches on the 9th May. The first 4 days were reasonably quiet and only 3 men were killed, but on the 13th the enemy shelled some detached outposts, demolishing them and causing several casualties. At 2pm they sent a bombing party down some disused communication trenches but this was driven back, and they tried this again without success. The Cheshires sent out a bombing party of their own inflicting casualties on the Germans.

At about 7pm the Germans exploded a mine in front of the British trenches and two attacks were launched by the Cheshires to secure the resulting crater. It was successful, but at some cost. The days action had resulted in the following casualty figures : 2 officers killed and 1 wounded, with 13 other ranks killed and 54 wounded. Andrew had got through the days fighting safely but 7 or 8 Wirral men had been killed, including James Owens from Bebington.

The following days activity (14th May) was simply reported by the diary as : *"Weather fine. Enemy artillery active all morning, but were very quiet during the night"* - no casualty figures were mentioned. Nevertheless, according to *"Soldiers Died in the Great War"* there were actually 5 men killed in action on the day and one of them was Andrew Dillon, aged 29.

Andrew has no known grave, but he is commemorated on the Arras memorial.

A poor photograph of the panel with his name on is shown on the following page. Almost 35,000 names of the "missing" are on this memorial.

Andrew qualified for a 1915 Star, British War Medal and Victory medal, and his wife Florrie would have received a Memorial Plaque and Scroll.

Andrew is also commemorated on the Bromborough Pool memorial at St. Matthew's church, both inside and outside the church.

THE WIRRAL PALS

For those readers with little knowledge of the Great War or the "Pals" Battalions a brief explanation is given here in order to give some background information to the following section of the book.

Many towns and cities raised volunteer "Pals" Battalions for their local Regiments, the idea being that men would be more likely to enlist if they knew that they would be serving with their friends and workmates.

Liverpool raised four Battalions (of approx. 1,000 men each) generally referred to as the Liverpool Pals, but officially they were the King's Liverpool 17th, 18th, 19th & 20th City Battalions.

Wirral only had one Pals Battalion, the 13th Battalion of the Cheshire Regiment. It was formed at Port Sunlight on 1st September 1914, and many of the first volunteers were Lever Brothers workers. At the first recruitment meeting in the Gladstone Hall, Port Sunlight about 500 men enlisted and just 6 days later on 7th September the Battalion marched through Chester now 700 strong. They were training at Sherrington Camp, Codford St. Mary near Bournemouth by December before moving to Aldershot in May 1915. They went to France on 25th September 1915, but due to depleted numbers they were eventually disbanded in France in February 1918. What men were left were transferred to other Battalions of the Cheshires.

Bebington lost at least 14 men from the original Pals Battalion :

Lr. Bebington : W/748 George Cooper, W/343 Andrew Dillon, W/816 William Forsey, W/282 George Inskip, W/198 Arthur Margerison, W/400 Samuel White ("Lancaster"), W/280 Percy Williams and W/879 William Wooliscroft.

Hr. Bebington : W/1115 James Owens, W/674 Henry Scheers, W/901 Ernest Smith, W/868 Frederick Smith, W/544 Charles Wilkins and W/469 Archie Williams.

The following pages give accounts for all of the Lower Bebington Pals who lost their lives in the war, with the exception of Andrew Dillon whose story is told with his brother Herbert. (see previous story).

W/816 PRIVATE WILLIAM FORSEY
13th Battalion Cheshire Regiment

WILLIAM FORSEY WAS BORN ON 20th July 1887 into a large and remarkably patriotic family. No less than seven brothers served in the Great War, but thankfully William was the only one to die.

The parents were Frederick and Sarah Jane Forsey and they were from the Dorset/Somerset area originally. They had married quite young and were living at Stretton near Warrington in 1881, and then at Brimstage Lane, Storeton in 1891. They had at least ten children before Frederick sadly passed away in 1897 aged just 41. The children in birth order were : Ellen, George, Frederick, Herbert, William, Frank, Florence, Harry, Colin, and Thomas.

Sarah and her children cannot be traced on the 1901 census and they may have been forced to split up, but in 1902 she married again to William Callanan an Irishman from Athenry near Galway in a civil ceremony in Wirral. They had two sons, John and William. Strangely Sarah was now calling herself Rhoda Callanan and this name was used on the 1911 census and by the Commonwealth War Graves Commission.

William was educated at Higher Bebington school, the family living at Storeton in the 1890's. On the 1911 census four of the brothers William, Frank, Colin and Thomas were still at home with their mother and step father at 12 Beverley Road, New Ferry. All four of them were earning their living at Lever Brothers, William employed as a Fettler's labourer. William Callanan was also working there.

He was a very keen footballer for Bebington St.Andrew's FC and also did his duties as a linesman for them.

Early in 1914 he married Harriet Lester at St. Mark's church in New Ferry, there didn't appear to be any children born of the marriage but no doubt the war was responsible for that.

On the outbreak of the war William didn't hesitate, enlisting with the 13th Battalion of the Cheshire Regiment early in September 1914. His brother Colin must have been just 3 behind him in the queue of volunteers judging by their service numbers!

Just like all the other locals who joined the Wirral Pals they did their training at Bournemouth and Aldershot before being posted overseas - arriving in France on 25th September 1915.

The following account is very similar to the one for Arthur Margerison, Arthur received fatal injuries on the same day that William Forsey was killed.

The "Pals" were at Zouave valley (about 8 miles north of Arras) during the last week or so of April 1916. They were in support lines on 27th but moved into the front line later in the day, 5 men being wounded in the process.

The following morning the Battalion were in the front line, and the war diary reported that the weather was very warm and the enemy artillery very active between 1pm and 2.45pm. At 7.10pm the enemy exploded a mine in front of the section of trench occupied by the 3rd Gloucesters and immediately occupied the crater. Soon after this the Cheshires were forced to withdraw a little, they were running short of ammunition and grenades and were suffering from heavy enfilade fire from the newly occupied crater. No wounded men were left behind. The trench they had been occupying was completely blown in by the enemy's trench mortars.

Casualty figures for the day were quoted as 4 officers wounded, 8 other ranks killed and 37 wounded. (*Soldiers Died in the Great War* gives 7 killed).

William, aged 28, was one of the 8 other ranks killed that day and his younger brother Colin was one of the wounded, receiving a bad head injury. Colin ended up in a London hospital but he eventually returned to the army, not being demobilised until May 1919. One of the others killed was 19 year old, W/413 Harold Clarke from Woodhead Street, New Ferry.

Going back to his six brothers who also served in the war a brief record of their service is given here :

W/8 Sgt. George Forsey : Cheshires
Frederick Forsey : Grenadier Guards
Frank Forsey : 18th Hussars
Sapper Harry Forsey : Cheshire Field Co. Royal Engineers
W/819 Pte. Colin Forsey : 13th Cheshires
Pte. Thomas Forsey : Cheshires

After William's death a photo of four of the brothers was printed in the Birkenhead News and it is reproduced here. In the centre are Colin and William, and it is believed to be Thomas on the left and George on the right.

William is buried in Ecoivres Military Cemetery and a photograph is shown here.

There are over 1,700 Commonwealth and nearly 800 French casualties in this cemetery.

William qualified for a 1915 Star, British War Medal, and Victory Medal. His wife Harriet would have received a Memorial Plaque and Scroll.

He is also commemorated on the Port Sunlight memorial.

W/198 PRIVATE ARTHUR MARGERISON
13th Battalion Cheshire Regiment

ARTHUR WAS BORN IN New Ferry on 27th April 1984, the son of Henry & Emily Jane Margerison. Emily was from Woolwich in Kent originally and Henry had been born locally, working as a "Timekeeper (Buildings)" in 1901, possibly at Lever Brothers.

The parents had married in Pimlico towards the end of 1871, but they had settled down in New Ferry by 1881. In 1901 and 1911 they had a nice company house at 73 Bolton Road, Port Sunlight (see photo).

There were eight children from the marriage but only five were alive by 1911. Those that have been traced were, in birth order : Peter, Henry, Frederick, Arthur, John (died aged 9) and Isaac.

Arthur has a very interesting story to tell, starting off with his schooling at the Port Sunlight village school. He had been a keen member of the Port Sunlight Boys Brigade (and in later years he was secretary of the Old Boys Association).

After his schooling he served an apprenticeship as a Compositor at Lever Brothers and was also a member of the Port Sunlight Silver Band. He eventually left Lever Brothers to work as a Printer at Messrs.Willmer Brothers.

Arthur was also a keen footballer and played outside left for Bebington St.Andrews A.F.C. for many years. There was an interesting report after a West Cheshire league game in the 1906-07 season which mentioned "- - - *another player having a number of free Saturdays was Bebington St. Andrew's Margerison, this for striking an opponent.*" - It seems to me that he would have been a good man to have beside you in a trench?

At this point it should also be mentioned that sadly Arthur's father Henry died in the first few months of the war aged 63.

Given what has already been said about Arthur it comes as no surprise to learn that (along with hundreds of other Port Sunlight men) he enlisted in the village in September 1914 with the 13th Battalion Cheshire Regiment (the "Wirral Pals").

After training in Bournemouth and Aldershot the 13th Battalion, Arthur, and many other local lads, were posted overseas - arriving in France on 25th September 1915.

The " Pals" were at Zouave valley (about 8 miles north of Arras) during the last week or so of April 1916, and Arthur had his 32nd birthday on 27th April. They were in support lines that morning but moved into the front line later in the day, 5 men were wounded in the process.

The following day the Battalion were in the front line, and the war diary reported that the weather was very warm and the enemy artillery very active between 1pm and 2.45pm. At 7.10pm the enemy exploded a mine in front of the section of trench occupied by the 3rd Gloucesters and immediately occupied the crater. Soon after this the Cheshires were forced to withdraw a little, they were running short of ammunition and grenades and were suffering from heavy enfilade fire from the newly occupied crater. No wounded men were left behind. The trench they had been occupying was completely blown in by the enemy's trench mortars.

Casualty figures for the day were quoted as 4 officers wounded, 8 other ranks killed and 37 wounded. (*Soldiers Died in the Great War* gives 7 killed).

It is likely that Arthur, one of the 37 wounded, received his fatal injury in the afternoon or early evening. However the *"Birkenhead News"* reported the incident in more detail.

It seems a German hand grenade (often called a "stick" grenade) dropped into the trench right by Arthur, he immediately grabbed it and threw it back out of the trench but it exploded before it had cleared the parapet of the trench. He was seriously wounded and taken to a casualty clearing station, but died of his wounds a few days later on 2nd May 1916, aged 32.

The day of Arthur's fatal injury was a bad one not just for the Wirral Pals who had a total of 7 or 8 men killed in action, but for 4 local men in particular who all died that day :

W/163 Richard Thompson of 31 Brunswick Street, Rock Ferry
W/413 Pte. Harold Clarke of 3 Woodhead Street, New Ferry.
W/476 Pte. William Jones of 24 St. Marys Gate, Birkenhead.
W/816 Pte. William Forsey of 12 Beverley Road, New Ferry.
William Forsey's brother Colin received a head wound the same day.

The tributes to Arthur after his death were profuse.

The tributes to Arthur after his death were profuse.

One friend in the Battalion, George Cooper, wrote to his mother :

"It is with regret I write these lines to tell you Arthur has been killed, he being wounded on the 28th of April and passing peacefully away at one of the clearing stations near us. We will have a cross put over his grave . . . . . he had little pain. In the few minutes he was conscious he asked me to let you know about him. We feel his loss very much, especially in the brass band, as he was a good player . . . . . Arthur was always cheerful, and always shared the contents of his parcels. Bill Forsey was killed and Colin Forsey wounded the night before Arthur was killed."

Alas, George Cooper was also to be killed a year later on 7th June 1917 and his story is told later in this book.

Arthur's Colonel also wrote to his mother, and included the remarkable tribute : *"Your son was one of the bravest and coolest men under fire that I have ever met."*

Arthur was buried in Aubigny Communal Cemetery Extension, there are nearly 2,800 Commonwealth burials from the Great War in this cemetery.

The epitaph simply reads: *"At Rest"*.

He is also commemorated on the Port Sunlight Memorial (albeit with a slight spelling error), and on the Boys Brigade Roll of Honour in Christ Church, Port Sunlight.

Arthur qualified for a 1915 Star, British War Medal, and Victory Medal. His mother would also have received a Memorial Plaque and Scroll.

W/282 PRIVATE GEORGE FREDERICK INSKIP
13th Battalion Cheshire Regiment

GEORGE'S PARENTS WERE WILLIAM INSKIP, a Labourer/Gardener from Stoke originally and local girl Martha. They married in Liverpool in 1886 and by 1891 they had settled down with their young family at No.9 Bromborough Road, Lower Bebington. They were still at the same address in 1911.

George himself was born in 1895, and the six children of the family in birth order were : Annie, Jessie, William, Samuel, George and Hannah Gertrude.

George was a member of the Church Lads Brigade, in Lower Bebington, and after his schooling he got a job as a Candle Wrapper – presumably at Prices in Bromborough Pool.

However he later started work at Lever Brothers, working in No.2 Soapery.

When war broke out George volunteered for the 13th Battalion Cheshire Regiment at Port Sunlight in early September 1914, along with his older brother Samuel (W/91) and brother-in-law J. Stocker (W/64) - who had married George's sister Jessie at St. Andrews on 3rd August 1914.

The three of them trained together, first in Bournemouth and then in Aldershot before the whole Battalion of Wirral Pals were posted to France – all of them arriving on 25th September 1915.

George had experienced the tough battles in April and May 1916 when Bebington men William Forsey, Arthur Margerison, James Owens, Andrew Dillon and Frederick Smith had all been killed. Then the Battle of the Somme started on 1st July and two more Bebington lads Archie Williams and Henry Scheers had also died. It really must have been very demoralising to the Infantrymen when so many were getting picked off month by month, but August was to be George's turn.

The Battalion were still on the Somme, at Mailly-Maillet about 5 miles north of Albert. On the 1st & 2nd August they were in trenches and suffered from heavy German shelling and 5 men had been killed.

On August 3rd the Battalion war diary reported directly on George's death (without actually naming him) :

"Quiet day. Casualties 1 killed and 9 wounded. These took place in Mailly Maillet Wood near the Quartermasters store, believed to be a bomb dropped by an aeroplane. Good work done."

George was the man killed, aged just 21. The Lever Brothers company magazine *"Progress"* added a bit more detail in their report of his death. He had been badly wounded by shrapnel from an aeroplane, and died on his way to hospital at Bertrancourt.

An officer, Lt. McFarland, wrote a sympathetic letter to his parents and included the compliment. *"He was eminently respected on account of his splendid disposition".*

George is buried in Bertrancourt Military Cemetery, only a couple of miles from Mailly-Maillet, and a photograph of his headstone is pictured alongside.

There are just over 400 casualties of the Great War here. The epitaph chosen by his parents reads :

"Gone to the Saints who from their labours rest on Jesu's breast"

George was awarded a 1915 Star, British War Medal, and Victory Medal. His parents also received a Memorial Plaque and Scroll.

He is also commemorated on the Port Sunlight memorial.

George's brother Samuel and brother-in-law John Stocker both survived the war and were demobilised in 1919.

W/879 PRIVATE WILLIAM HENRY WOOLISCROFT
13th Battalion Cheshire Regiment

WILLIAM WOOLISCROFT IS A BIT of a mystery man, there was absolutely nothing in the local newspapers about his time in the army and even on the original paperwork for the memorial in the early 1920's his name was spelt as both Woolliscroft and Wolliscroft. On the actual memorial tablet he is shown as Woolliscroft. However the correct spelling is Wooliscroft, according to his birth and marriage certificates.

William was born in the All Saints district of Birmingham on the 27th December 1895, the son of Joseph and Emily Wooliscroft. Joseph was originally from Rossett and after marrying Emily (who was from Birmingham) they settled down there for a while. Joseph was working as a Groom in 1891 and an Ostler (or Stableman) on William's marriage certificate in 1915.

According to the original paperwork about the memorial from the 1920's William's next of kin lived at Rossett (between Chester and Wrexham) – see below :

William H.Wolliscroft, -✔   Relatives live at Rossett. Mrs.Feightmann
                             56 Oakleigh Grove. would forward.

William was living at Burton near Rossett on the 1901 and 1911 censuses, and in 1911 they were at Rosemary Lane, Burton. Joseph was now a widower. William was 17 and working as a Groom. There were three surviving children of the marriage in 1911, Rosy (possibly Emily Rose), William and Arthur

81

Using the scanty information given above, the only likely man to have died in the Great War would be No. W/879 in the 13th Battalion of the Cheshires.

After speaking to an authority on the Battalion it is also known that William attested to the Wirral Pals early in September 1914 and served with No.2 Company. At the time of his enlistment his sister was living at South View, Bromborough Pool (this must have been Rosy) and perhaps William was living there too?

At the risk of repeating the information given for many other Wirral Pals who are in this book William trained at Bournemouth first and then at Malplaquet Barracks in Aldershot before embarking for France and arriving there on 25th September 1915.

The big difference between William and all the other local lads in the Battalion who were training on the south coast was that he met and married a girl from the Bournemouth area.

They were only training in Bournemouth from December to May, but that was long enough for William to find a girl and on Friday 10th September 1915 he married Elizabeth Stringer from Pokesdown, Bournemouth at the Register Office in Christchurch. According to his birth certificate he was 19 years old, but it says 25 on the marriage certificate. Perhaps he didn't want to give his real age because his wife was actually quite a bit older at 29. Just 15 days later he was in France.

As explained in the stories of other men from the 13th Battalion, they had a very tough time in 1916. Many Bebington men were casualties between April and August, and eight had been killed. William had come through all this and he was still there in October.

It was getting toward the tail end of the Somme campaign, 20th October 1916, and the Battalion were between Martinpuich and Thiepval.

They took up a front line position in Hessian trench, and there was to be an attack on a German position known as Regina trench the following morning.

The war diary reported that on Saturday 21st after a preliminary barrage the whole Battalion went over the top just after noon *"with the greatest gallantry"* and advanced behind a rolling barrage. They entered the German trench without much difficulty, capturing about 250 prisoners plus a machine gun and also putting a German field gun out of action. They then consolidated their position and were eventually relieved at 3pm on the 22nd.

The attack was rightly seen as a huge success but it was also at a great cost.
    The war diary gave the casualty figures :
    3 officers and 74 other ranks killed, 7 officers and 116 other ranks wounded, with 2 officers and 56 other ranks missing.
    Charles Amer of New Ferry was one of those killed.

William died of wounds on 23rd October, but he almost certainly received these wounds during the big attack on the 21st.
    According to his birth certificate he was just 20 years old, but his headstone says 27. This anomaly could have been something to do with the incorrect age given on his marriage certificate.

William qualified for a 1915 Star, British War Medal, and Victory Medal.
    His wife Elizabeth would have also received a Memorial Plaque and Scroll.

He is buried in Contay British Cemetery, and there are over 1,100 Commonwealth casualties from the Great War buried here.
    A photo of his headstone is shown here, his wife Elizabeth chose his epitaph of :

"Sadly missed by his loving wife and son"

And there lies the rub. George had married Elizabeth before going off to the war (as so many other soldiers did) but he also knew that she was pregnant, and his son also called William arrived early in 1916. Sadly it is very doubtful that he ever saw him.

There is a Pte. W.Wooliscroft in the Lever Brothers *"Golden Book"* of those who served in the war, but he is not shown as being killed. He is not named on the Port Sunlight Memorial either, but it is possible that it is him all the same – not all of the casualties were notified to the Company.

W/748 PRIVATE GEORGE COOPER
13th Battalion – Cheshire Regiment

GEORGE WAS BORN IN MALPAS in 1891, one of seven children of Charles and Martha Cooper (both also from the Malpas area originally). Charles was an Agricultural Labourer on the 1891 census and the family were living at Wigland near Malpas. Charles appears to have died in the 1890's, and Martha eventually married again to Philip Fox about 1898.

The children from the first marriage were Albert, Mary, Jane Annie, Ellis, Alexander and George and Eunice.

In 1901 Alexander, George and Eunice were living with their mother and step father in Bickerstaffe, West Lancashire.

George had set out on his own before the next census in 1911 when he was 20 years old and living as a boarder with the Ebbrell family at 12 Park Road, Port Sunlight. Charles Ebbrell also 20, the son of the house, probably arranged Georges "digs" because they were both employed as packers in the advertising warehouse at Lever Brothers. (Charles immigrated to Australia in 1912, and fought with the Australians in Gallipoli, Egypt, and the Western Front).

Conveniently, the house was just a couple of minutes walk from the main factory entrance. George attended the Wesleyan church in Lower Bebington.

He enlisted with the 13th Battalion of the Cheshire Regiment at Port Sunlight on 5th September 1914, serving in No.3 company. After training in Bournemouth and Aldershot the 13th Battalion, George included, were posted overseas - arriving in France on 25th September 1915.

George was in the thick of it near Arras at the end of April 1916. On the 28th Harold Clarke and William Forsey from New Ferry were both killed and Arthur Margerison received a fatal wound. George wrote a lovely letter to Arthur's mother which is quoted in Arthur's story earlier in the book. William Forsey's story also appears here.

George carried on, he had lost some good friends from Port Sunlight in 1916 but the fighting continued endlessly on the Western Front.

He has no service records, but seems to have escaped injury until June 1917.

The Wirral Pals were about to get involved in the Battle of Messines in Belgium, and they spent several days preparing for a major attack planned for the 7th June. The Battalion war diary reported that they had moved off to their assembly trenches the night before the attack.

At 3.10 am a series of 19 huge mines were detonated under the German lines, and the British artillery opened up a devastating barrage.

The Pals went over the top immediately and everything went according to plan. Very little opposition was encountered except in a few cases when German machine guns opened from a flank, and these were swiftly dealt with. The action was all over in a few hours and the rest of the day was reported to be quiet: *"the enemy being so disorganised that his shelling was wild and ineffective. No German counter attack was launched".*

It makes it sound like a piece of cake, and the Battle of Messines in 1917 actually was a big success - but the 13th Cheshires casualties on the first day don't make good reading.

The war diary mentions 2 officers killed and 4 wounded, with 29 other ranks killed, 132 wounded, and 15 missing.

George was one of those killed in action, probably by machine gun fire, aged 26. Also among the dead that day were local men W/1122 Bertie Woods from Lever Bros. and 243732 Joseph Woodfin from Rock Ferry.

George has no known grave, but he is one of the 54,000+ men commemorated on the Menin Gate in Ypres, and a photo of the panel showing his name is shown here.

He qualified for a 1915 Star, British War Medal and Victory Medal, and his mother should have received a Memorial Plaque and Scroll.

He is also commemorated on the Lever Brothers memorial and the Wesleyan memorial in Lower Bebington.

As a footnote, George's mother moved around during and after the war, perhaps due to her husbands farm work. She had a couple of later addresses : Berry Cottage, Bridge Trafford near Chester, and Manor Cottage, Noctorum, Birkenhead.

CHESHIRE	REGIMENT
PRIVATE	PRIVATE
ARMSTRONG O.	COLLINS F.
ARNOLD B.	COLLINS F A.
ASHCROFT A. O.	COLMAN W.
ASHPITAL J. W.	COMBOY M.
ASHTON J.	COOK A.
ASHTON R.	COOK A.P.
ASHTON T.	COOKSON W. H.
ASTON J.	COOP A.
BAGLEY T.	COOPER E.W.
BAGWELL H.	COOPER F.
BAIGENT W. E.	COOPER G.
BAILEY E.	COOPER W. T.
BAILEY F.	CORRIGAN J.

W/400 PRIVATE SAMUEL WHITE ("LANCASTER")
13ᵗʰ + 10ᵗʰ Battalions - Cheshire Regiment

THE MORE ALERT READER MAY well be thinking *"I don't remember seeing a Samuel White on the memorial tablet"* - well the short answer is that there isn't !

It had been proving impossible to find one of the other men on the memorial, namely Samuel Lancaster. There was no casualty of that name to be found with links to Bebington.

Fortunately a good family historian came to the writers rescue with the all so simple answer to the problem.

Samuel White was born out of wedlock to Margaret Annie White late 1884 or early 1885. Very soon after Margaret married Peter Lancaster at St.Andrew's Bebington in the spring of 1885.

The couple were living at No.10 Lunar Street, Tranmere in 1891, Peter being a house painter. They had Samuel with them and had added two other sons, Peter and Thomas. Everyone on the census, including Samuel, was named Lancaster, as they were in 1901 when they were at 16 Comet Street – with the latest additions of Joseph and Aaron. Samuel was 16 now and working as an Errand Boy in the Docks. Peter was always working as a house painter, and in 1911 the parents were living at No.8 Oakleigh Grove with Joseph, Aaron and young Margaret Annie.

Samuel was not at home now because he had got married (under the name of Samuel White) to Jane Perry at St. Paul's church in Tranmere in the spring of 1908. In 1911 they were living at No.54 Rochester Road, Rock Ferry and had a 1 year old daughter Jane. Samuel was working as a Labourer in a Timber Yard at this time but shortly after he got a job at Lever Brothers, working in the Timber Store. By the time he enlisted the family were living at 220 New Chester Road, Port Sunlight (see photo) Samuel and Jane eventually had four children : Jane, Samuel, Maggie, and finally Alfred in March 1916.

Samuel was one of the original volunteers for the Wirral Pals Battalion of the Cheshire Regiment, enlisting as W/400 Private Samuel

White, early in September 1914. He was posted to No.3 Company and commenced training at Sherrington Camp, Bournemouth, later moving to Aldershot.

On 25th September 1915 the whole Battalion embarked at Southampton for France, arriving there later the same day.

Samuel was serving with many other Wirral men in the Pals, and accounts of the Bebington men who died are either in this book or in *"Higher Bebington's Heroes 1914 -1919".*

Suffice to say, he would almost certainly have been involved in the actions at Zouave Valley (near Vimy) - where Bebington men William Forsey, Arthur Margerison, James Owens, Andrew Dillon and Fred Smith had all been killed.

Ovillers - where Archie Williams was killed.

Mailly-Maillet - George Inskip.

Thiepval - William Wooliscroft.

Messines - George Cooper.

Passchendaele - Ernest Smith.

All 10 of these were Bebington men, and almost all of them had worked at Lever Brothers. Truly, they were all Wirral Pals.

Samuel had served in the Pals since day one and he was still there when they were disbanded in France on 16th February 1918. It must have been a sad day for those who, like Samuel, had come through it all. However the war was far from over and many of the Pals were transferred to the 10th Battalion of the Cheshires, Samuel was one of them.

The following month, 21st March, the Germans launched their Spring Offensive and it was to be Samuel's undoing.

The Battalion were at Achiet-le-Grand on the 21st, about 3 miles north west of the town of Bapaume on the Somme.

The Battalion were in the thick of it from the 21st – 26th March and had 2 officers and 51 men killed, with very many more wounded or missing.

Samuel was killed in action on 24th March 1918 at the age of 33. There is no other details about his death but it was reported in the war diary on the evening of the 24th that : *"the Battalion by this time were thoroughly disorganised. All the Company Commanders and many other officers had become casualties".*

It comes as no surprise then, given the desperate circumstances prevailing at the time, that Samuel has no known grave and is commemorated on the Arras memorial.

A poor quality photograph of his name is shown here.

There are nearly 35,000 Commonwealth soldiers listed on this memorial to the missing all of them killed between Spring 1916 and August 1918.

Samuel is also commemorated on the Port Sunlight Memorial under the name of S.White.

He was awarded a 1915 Star, British War Medal and Victory Medal.

His widow Jane would also have received a Memorial Plaque and Scroll.

Samuel had two brothers, or half brothers, serving in the war :

31084 Pte. Aaron Lancaster : East Lancashire Regiment : Taken prisoner in March 1918 aged 19 but survived the war. (see photo)

And also Joseph Lancaster : Married with 2 children : Served in France, survived the war.

W/280 + 268092 PRIVATE PERCY WILLIAMS
13th + 10th Battalions Cheshire Regiment

PERCY WAS BORN IN SPITAL on 15th December 1893, the youngest of six children born to Thomas Richardson Williams and his wife Sarah.

Thomas was from Wallasey originally, and he had married a Bebington girl Sarah Whitehead at St. Mary's in Birkenhead towards the end of 1878. The children of the marriage in birth order were :
William, Frank Richardson, Sarah Ann, Fred, May and Percy.

The family were living at 26 Oakleigh Grove, Lower Bebington on the 1901 & 1911 censuses and Thomas was working as a Cotton Warehouseman or Porter. By wartime he was employed as an assistant in the timber department of Lever Brothers and Percy was also working there as in the No.2 Woodbox Department.

When war was declared he was one of the first to join up, as W/280 Private Percy Williams in September 1914. He joined the 13th

Cheshires (Wirral Pals), training with them in Bournemouth and Aldershot before the whole Battalion were posted to France, arriving there on 26th September 1915.

It is known that he received serious injuries to both of his shoulders in August 1917, and he spent several months recuperating. At least part of it was in a convalescent home in Manchester, and the Lever Brothers company magazine reported that he was still there in December.

The 13th Battalion was disbanded in France on 16th February 1918 and many of the men were transferred to the 10th Battalion. Percy's service record has not survived but he was most likely one of this group.

He was with the 10th Battalion in March 1918 though, and it was the time of the German Spring Offensive. On 21st March the Germans had a last throw of the dice and attacked for all they were worth, they wanted to win the war before the large number of American troops arriving in France could help sway the balance in the Allies favour.

The 10th Cheshires were at Achiet-le Grand on the 21st, about 3 miles north west of the town of Bapaume on the Somme.

The Battalion were in the thick of it from the 21st – 26th March and had 2 officers and 51 men killed, with very many more wounded or missing.

Percy was actually posted as "missing" on the 27th and yet on the night of the 26th/27th what was left of the Battalion had marched back to billets in Couin.

It is possible that Percy may have been killed a day or two earlier because the war diary commented on the evening of the 24th that: *"the Battalion by this time were thoroughly disorganised. All the company commanders and many other officers had become casualties".*

So it may not have been realised that Percy actually was missing, such was the situation at that time.

Officially Percy was killed in action on the 27th aged 24, but he has no known grave and is commemorated on the Arras memorial. He is not alone though, there are nearly 35,000 Commonwealth soldiers listed on this memorial to the missing all of them killed between Spring 1916 and August 1918.

He is also commemorated on the Port Sunlight Memorial and was awarded a 1915 Star, British War Medal and Victory Medal.
Never having married, his parents would have received a Memorial Plaque and Scroll.

As a point of local interest, Samuel White ("Lancaster") of the same Battalion was killed a few days earlier on the 24th. His story is told earlier in the book.

63520 PRIVATE JOSEPH MULLRAY
6th Labour Company - Kings Liverpool Regiment

ACCORDING TO THE 1911 CENSUS Joseph was born in New Ferry in 1878, and he was living at No.8 Willow Bank Road in New Ferry with his wife Lucy and children Jenny and Eileen. There is no trace of him on previous censuses, so that part of his story remains a mystery.

He was working as a Labourer in Lever Brothers Soapworks, and had 17 years service in before he joined the army. At the time of volunteering he was working in the printing department.

He had married Lucy Jerram Wilson at Birkenhead early in 1902. By 1917 they were living at 30 Trafalgar Drive, Lower Bebington.

He enlisted on 15th February 1917 at Bebington, and seems to have been posted overseas to the 6th Labour company of the Kings

Liverpool Regiment. Possibly at his enlistment age of 39 the army didn't consider him fit for the infantry?

His service papers have not survived, so little else is known about Joseph's short army career other than that his health broke down within months of arriving in France. He was taken to No.2 Casualty Clearing Station and died of diabetes on May 10th at the age of 39.

Joseph is buried in Barlin Communal Cemetery Extension, south of Bethune. It contains almost 1,100 Commonwealth burials from the Great War.

The epitaph, chosen by his wife reads :

"Dearer to memory than words can tell. His lonely wife and children"

Joseph is also commemorated on the Port Sunlight memorial, and was awarded a British War Medal and Victory medal, and his wife would also have received a Memorial Plaque and Scroll.

15260 PRIVATE ARTHUR NEVITT
8th Battalion South Lancashire Regiment

ARTHUR WAS ONE OF TEN children born to William Henry and Sarah Nevitt. William was a farm worker from Whitchurch in Shropshire originally, and his wife was born in Malpas. They married about 1888 but on the 1901 census they were living at "Smithy Cottage" in Poulton-cum-Spital. They were at "Claremont Cottage" in 1911 and this would probably have been a cottage tied to Claremont Farm. There is a possibility that it was the same house as 1901.

They had 9 surviving children in 1911 and in birth order they were: Thomas, Elizabeth, Harry, Joseph, Arthur, Ellis, Elsie, Hilda and Frances.

Arthur himself was born in the Chester area about February 1895. In 1911 he was unemployed but had been working as an under gardener. However, his older brother Joseph was working at Lever Brothers and perhaps this was a help to him in securing a job there himself. He was 19 years old and working in No.2 Soapery (Frame Room) when war was declared, but he wasted little time in volunteering for the Cheshires at Birkenhead on 4th September 1914 as 16479 Private Arthur Nevitt. His medical reveals that he was 5'-6 ¾" tall, 9 stone 2lbs, with blue eyes, light brown hair and sallow complexion. He was also Church of England.

For some reason he was transferred to the 8th Battalion South Lancashires ten days later, and after training with them in the UK for a year he was posted overseas, arriving in France on 28th September 1915.

He was at the Somme in 1916 and was out of action for a while after being wounded.

The following year he was granted a few days leave in June, but had not long been back at the front when he was killed on 1st August 1917 aged 22.

The 3rd Battle of Ypres was raging (commonly known as Passchendaele) and the Battalion war diary reported that they were at Westhoek Ridge, moving into assembly positions on 31st July.

On the 1st August at 2pm, while the South Lancs were moving into the front line, the enemy counter attacked and drove the 2nd Middlesex Regt back. "D" company of the South Lancs repulsed this attack and fought their way back to the position left by the Middlesex. By 8pm the rest of the Battalion had joined "D" company in their front line position.

At some point in the days proceedings Arthur was killed in action aged 22, the only man killed on that day. No more detail of his death can be found, but he has no known grave and so he is yet another Bebington man commemorated on the Menin Gate at Ypres. A photo of the panel with his name on it is shown on the next page.

Arthur qualified for a 1915 Star, British War Medal and Victory Medal. His parents also received a Memorial Plaque and Scroll.

He is also commemorated on the Port Sunlight memorial.

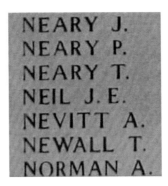

NEARY J.
NEARY P.
NEARY T.
NEIL J. E.
NEVITT A.
NEWALL T.
NORMAN A.

Arthur's four brothers also served in the war, and a photograph of all five of them appeared in the *"Birkenhead News"* in May 1917 and the photo is shown below. The photo is faked, Arthur has certainly been superimposed in the centre.

Top left is Thomas who was in the Royal Welsh Fusiliers well before the war and was wounded in the retreat from Mons.

Top right is Joseph, also in the Royal Welsh Fusiliers and wounded at Loos.

Bottom left is Harry of the Royal Field Artillery.

Bottom right is Ellis who was wounded with the 4th Cheshires at Gallipoli, later also serving with the Royal Welsh Fusiliers.

2ND LIEUTENANT RALPH ROYDS BROCKLEBANK
1st Battalion – Royal Welsh Fusiliers

RALPH WAS FROM A VERY well to do family, his father Ralph Eric Brocklebank had been a Major in the 6th Kings Liverpool Regiment, he was a Justice of the Peace and owner or director of several businesses including J.P. Higginson (Coal Merchants) of Water Street in Liverpool, Mersey Coal Elevators, and West Appleton Rubber Plantations.

Ralph's mother was Constance Alington Brocklebanks, the daughter of the Rev. Nathaniel Royds – hence Ralph's unusual middle name?

The family were living at "Poulton Royd" Spital, Bebington in the 1901 and 1911 censuses and they were still there in the 1920's. This is a magnificent 15 room house, complete with wonderful gardens and the Brocklebanks were employing 3 or 4 servants. The house is situated right next door to Claremont Farm, which is a popular "pick your own strawberries" place with a good farm shop these days.

The seven children of the marriage, in birth order, appear to be Ralph, Denys, Peter, Richard Philip, Elsie Mary (died aged 1), Giles and Thomas Christopher – all of them having the middle name of Royds!

Ralph was born in Bebington on 21st June 1897 and was destined to have a first class education. Starting at Cordwalles prep school in Maidenhead, followed by Eton College – no wonder he couldn't be found on the 1911 census.

He was an excellent sportsman, playing rugby and cricket, a good swimmer, and he rowed for Eton. In his service papers it was noted that he stood 6'- 4" tall at the age of just 16.

He attended the Royal Military College, Sandhurst in 1915 and was gazetted as a 2nd Lieutenant on 22nd December 1915.

Ralph suffered a nasty injury caused by a hand grenade in training on 18th June 1916, resulting in the loss of his right thumb and forefinger, which is why he wasn't posted out to France until 10th January 1917 as a 2nd Lt. with the 1st Battalion Royal Welsh Fusiliers.

An interesting point to mention here is that on 30th December 1916 - just a fortnight before Ralph left for France, the famous war poet Siegfried Sassoon visited "Poulton Royd".

In the published diaries of Siegfried Sassoon (edited by Rupert Harte-Davis) there is a note that after a disappointing days fox hunting at Tiverton near Tarporley he (Sassoon) – *"Went back to Beeston Station and on to Spital with Brocklebank, and had a cheery evening at his home. Back to the huts at 12"*.

The published diary indicates that it was young Ralph he visited, not his father.

The next day Sassoon played golf at Formby with Robert Graves, a fellow poet.

In May 1917 the 1ˢᵗ Royal Welsh Fusiliers were in the Battle of Arras, and on 14th May they were attacking German positions in Bullecourt village. The attack commenced at 2.10am but despite much fierce fighting the attack was called off by 10am. In the mornings fighting they had 3 Officers and 14 Other Ranks killed and Ralph received a serious leg wound.

He was taken to No. 49 casualty clearing station and the following day he had his leg amputated, dying the day after, aged just 19.

He is buried in Achiet-le-Grande Cemetery which contains over 1,400 Commonwealth burials, a photo is shown here.

The epitaph reads :
"He asked life of thee and thou gavest
him a long life even for ever & ever"

Ralph was awarded a British War Medal and Victory Medal, and his parents would have received a Memorial Plaque and Scroll.

Ralphs younger brother Denys served in the war as a Sub Lieutenant in the Royal Navy and won a British War Medal and Victory Medal.

4463 PRIVATE JOHN DAWBER
2nd Regiment South African Infantry

JOHN WAS BORN IN WARRINGTON towards the end of 1881, the son of John and Jane Dawber. John senior was a General Labourer at that time but at some point between the 1891 census and 1901 he had joined Lever Brothers Soapworks and was employed there as a Foreman. The family had a beautiful Company house (see photo) at No.10 Riverside, barely a five minute walk from the factory and they now had six children : Mary, Peter, Richard, John, Annie and Rhoda.

In 1911 they were still living at 10 Riverside, but only had three children at home.

Jack, as he was popularly known, was now aged about 30, he had joined Lever Brothers straight from school and was working as a Soap Cutter in 1901. The company offered him a position at their Durban works in South Africa and he took it, working there as a Foreman.

This was probably before 1911 because he wasn't at home on the census, and he had never married.

On August 24th 1915 he joined the South African Infantry, his papers give an enlistment date of 3rd September at Potchefstroom, near Johannesburg.

His medical revealed that he was 5'-8½" tall, 10½ stone, with a pale complexion, grey brown eyes and dark brown hair. He was also C. of E.

It is not clear where Jack did his training but having spent Christmas 1915 in the UK he boarded the transport ship *"Saxonia"* at Devonport on 29th December. He was with "A" company of the 2nd South African Infantry, bound for Alexandria in Egypt disembarking there on 12th January.

He served exactly 3 months along the Egyptian coast before boarding the *"Megantic"* at Alexandria and landing at Marseille on 20th April 1916. His next major stop would be the Somme.

In July 1916 the South African Infantry were fighting at the Somme and they were involved in the infamous attack on Delville Wood near Longueval. They joined the attack on the 15th July and held on to their position in the wood for several days despite terrific casualties. To give an idea of the situation an extract from *"The Official History of the Great War 1914-1918"* is quoted here.

"The South Africans had covered themselves with glory at Delville Wood. In spite of terrible losses, they had steadfastly endured the ordeal of the German bombardment, which seldom slackened and never ceased, and had faced with great courage and resolution repeated counter-attacks delivered by fresh German troops. Since their first advance into the wood

on the morning of 15th July they had defied all attempts to drive them completely from it".

The South Africans had gone into battle on the 15th July with 121 officers and 3,032 other ranks. At roll call on 21st July they numbered only 29 officers and 751 other ranks.

Jack suffered a gunshot wound to the right knee on the 16th and was transferred to a hospital at Le Havre. He was then taken back to the UK on board the *"Dunluce Castle"* on 21st July. He ended up at the 4th London General Hospital, Denmark Hill on the 23rd and he was diagnosed with a fractured kneecap. His wound was reported to be only *"slight"* but then a week later he was taken *"seriously ill."* His condition must have improved over the next couple of months but he took another turn for the worse and died on October 23rd aged 35.

His body was brought back to the Wirral and after a service in Christ Church, Port Sunlight he was buried with full military honours in Bebington Cemetery.

The coffin, draped in the Union Jack, was conveyed on a gun carriage first to the church and then on to the cemetery. The Band of the Cheshire Regiment accompanied the procession and the "Last Post" was sounded after three volleys had been fired over the grave.

Jack is also commemorated on the Port Sunlight memorial and on the Wesleyan memorial in Lower Bebington.

He qualified for a British War Medal and Victory Medal, which were only posted out to his parents in October 1925. They would also have received a Memorial Plaque and Scroll.

There is an error on Jack's Commonwealth War Graves headstone. The badge shown is for the Royal Navy and not the South African badge with a Springboks head on it. It is unbelievable that this has gone unnoticed for over 90 years, the CWGC have been informed and the headstone should be replaced in the next 12 months or so.

35734 PRIVATE WILLIAM ALEXANDER BROWN
1/4th Battalion – King's Shropshire Light Infantry

WILLIAM WAS BORN IN BOOTLE near Liverpool in the second quarter of 1899. His parents William and Helen were both born near Dumfries and were probably married in Scotland, but in 1897/8 they had moved down to Liverpool with their first child.

They were living at 27 Keats Street, Bootle and over the next 10 years they had five more children. They were still in Bootle in 1911, but living at 4 Mary Road now.

The six children in birth order were Janet, Mary, William Alexander, George, Elsie and Alfred.

William senior had been a Dock Labourer in 1901 but on the 1911 census he was working as an Electrical Signal Fitter on the Liverpool overhead railway. Young William was attending Orrell Council School and was head boy there. (A rather poor photo of him in wartime is shown here.)

At some point between 1911 and 1916 his parents moved to 62 Bolton Road in Port Sunlight. His father must have started work at

Lever Brothers because the family were living in a nice company house. William junior started work at Levers too, working as a forwarding clerk in the main office.

No service records have survived for William so there is nothing to indicate when he actually joined up. Although many boys did enlist under age, strictly speaking he would not have been required to join the army until perhaps early 1917.

When he did join up he probably trained with the Cheshires (and Lever Brothers magazine did mistakenly report him as being with the Cheshires when he died). Having spoken to an expert on the Kings Shropshire Light Infantry (referred to as KSLI from now on) it seems highly probable that he was transferred to them about 25th March 1918 and sent over to France on 28th March as part of a reinforcement draft.

The following details are based on an excellent account of the Battalion's movements at the end of May & beginning of June 1918 given on the Shropshire Regimental Museum website.

After the German Spring Offensive in March and April 1918 things were a lot quieter on the British Front during May, but the Germans had switched their attention to the French sector further south. In order to assist the French some British troops, including the 4th KSLI, were sent to help.

The Battalion were sent by train via Paris to Rheims and spent a few weeks behind the line whilst receiving drafts of new recruits to make up their full strength. This may well have included the arrival of William.

On May 28th the Germans attacked in strength between the Marne and the Aisne, and the 4th KSLI were hurried into action to meet them. Over the next few days the British were pushed back from Chambrecy, and suffered heavy casualties. By the 5th June the Shropshires were down to just 350 men, a Temporary Commanding Officer and seven Junior Officers.

The 9th Cheshires and 8th North Staffordshires were holding Bligny Hill with the KSLI in reserve a mile in the rear at Chaumuzy. The hill was heavily shelled and gassed on the night of 5th and the Germans launched an attack at 6am the following morning (6th June).

By 8am the North Staffs and Cheshires were taking heavy casualties on Bligny Hill and their wounded were streaming back towards Chaumuzy. The Germans had taken the hill by mid morning and the 4th KSLI were ordered to launch a counter attack on the hill at 12.45pm, the aim was to retake the hill and drive off the German defenders. They advanced in 3 waves with a 4th in reserve.

They crossed a mile of corn fields in full view of the Germans on the hill, but as soon as the 1st wave set off they suffered shrapnel shelling. Machine gun and rifle fire opened up when they reached the base of the hill. Approximately 200 Shropshires were in the attack and it was estimated that 80 were casualties by the time they reached the hill.

Lt. G.W. Bright then led 3 lines of the KSLI (plus the remnants of the Cheshires & North Staffs making up a 4th line) in an attack straight up the hill.

The first wave was in the German trenches within 5 minutes, and as the other waves arrived at least 30 Germans surrendered and the rest fled the hill but retained a foothold at its base.

At this point the KSLI were down to about 100 fit men, but they nevertheless held the hill all evening and night despite shrapnel shelling and sniping before eventually being relieved by the Northumberland Fusiliers.

Sadly, at some point in the fighting on the 6th June William had been seriously wounded. He was removed to a casualty clearing station, and eventually to a hospital near Rouen where he died of his wounds about 5 weeks later on 12th July 1918 at the age of just 19.

He is buried in St. Sever Cemetery Extension, Rouen. There are over 8,000 Commonwealth casualties of the Great War here, the vast majority of them would have died in one of several hospitals in the Rouen area.

The epitaph chosen by his parents reads :

"When the day dawns we shall meet again"

William qualified for a British War Medal and Victory Medal and his parents would have received a Memorial Plaque and Scroll.

He is also commemorated on the Port Sunlight memorial.

The attack on Bligny Hill had been witnessed by the French General Berthelot, who was so impressed with the 4th KSLI that he immediately authorised the award of a Croix de Guerre with Palm to the whole Battalion.

28534 PRIVATE JOHN GEE
1/5th Battalion Border Regiment

JOHN WAS BORN IN 1890 and his family were from Welshampton in Shropshire originally, but moved to Bebington sometime after 1903. They lived at 16 Trafalgar Place (also referred to as Ash Grove). This address no longer exists but using the local census summary of 1911 it would have been between Trafalgar Drive and the Wiend, very close to St. Andrews church. His parents were Thomas, a cow man or farm labourer, and Sarah. They had six children, all boys, Henry, John, Thomas William, Edwin, James Albert and Herbert Douglas. In 1911 the father and 3 of their sons (John included) were all working on one of the local farms – perhaps at Spital?

However John soon gave up his farm work and started work at Lever Brothers in the cotton seed mill.

It is difficult to be precise about John's army career because his service and pension records have not survived and only his medal index card exists.

From this we find out that he served overseas with three regiments, first as 36353 in the South Wales Borderers, then 43591 with the Kings Liverpool, and finally with the 1/5th (Cumberland) Battalion of the Border Regiment. All this in the space of 13 months.

The "Birkenhead News" report on his death mentions that he joined the Scottish Borderers in 1915 and was posted to France with them in February 1917. This was probably an error and should have read South Wales Borderers.

Little more is known other than that in March 1918 he was taken prisoner, this was most likely during the German Spring offensive in France.

Looking at the Battalions casualty figures for the month we find that they lost 87 officers and men in March, all of them between the 21st and 30th - and 58 of them were on the 21st of March. It looks quite probable that John may have been taken prisoner on that day.

He was held in a prisoner of war camp in Germany, but died on 6th July 1918 at the age of 28.

It is not known if this was as a result of any injuries he may have received in March or whether it was natural causes.

Interestingly the Commonwealth War Graves Commission report that over the course of the Great War almost 300,000 Commonwealth servicemen were taken prisoner on the Western Front. Most of these were held in camps in Germany, and approximately 12,000 died in captivity.

John's younger brother Edwin enlisted with the Royal Welsh Fusiliers in October 1916 aged 18 but did not see overseas service.

John is buried in Cologne Southern Cemetery. Nearly 2,500

Commonwealth service men are buried here. The majority were POW's who, like John, died in the German POW camps.

John was awarded the British War Medal and the Victory Medal and his parents would have received a Memorial Plaque and Scroll.

He is also commemorated on the Port Sunlight memorial.

94247 PRIVATE THOMAS ALFRED EVANS
17th Kings Liverpool Regiment

CHRISTENED THOMAS ALFRED EVANS, he was born in the final quarter of 1898. From that point on everyone dropped the *"Thomas"* bit and everyone knew him simply as Alfred Evans.

He was one of seven surviving children of Joseph & Alice Evans on the 1911 census. Joseph always being employed as a Cowman on a farm. He and Alice were from Welshampton in Shropshire originally but moved to Wirral in the 1880's, all of their children were born in Bromborough and were, in birth order : William, Annie, Alfred, Lilian, Hilda, Ada and Doris.

The family were living at 3 Pool-lane Cottages in some newspaper reports, This was probably the present day Pool Lane in Bromborough Pool. There are no cottages there nowadays though.

Young Alfred was only 12 on the 1911 census and listed as a schoolboy. His two older siblings were working at Prices Candle

Works now. Alfred also started work there after he left school, getting in 4½ years service - mainly in the sawmill.

Alfred joined the Kings Liverpool Regiment, on March 26th 1917 at the age of 18. After training he was posted overseas and arrived in France on 17th March 1918, to *"D"* company of the 17th Battalion (1st Liverpool Pals).

The Germans had launched their Spring Offensive on 21st March, it was a last great effort on their part to win the war before the large numbers of American troops swung the war in the Allies favour. The British were resisting as best they could and the 17th Kings were at Voormezeele (about 4 miles south of Ypres) on 29th April.

The war diary reported : *"At 3.30am a heavy enemy bombardment opened, followed later by enemy attack, and our line was forced back - - - - - the enemy got through on both flanks practically surrounding 2 companies. "A" company was surrounded and after severe fighting were captured."*

Alfred was reported missing on this day, and nothing definite was ever heard of what had happened to him. Indeed his parents were placing tributes in the Birkenhead News for years after.

The one shown here is from the edition dated 30th April 1921.

EVANS.—In loving memory of our dear son, Pte. ALFRED EVANS, who was missing 29th April, 1918, now presumed killed.
A loving son, a brother kind,
A beautiful memory left behind.
He bravely answered his country's call,
His life he gave for one and all.
Beloved son of J. and A. Evans, 3, Pool-lane Cottage

Commonwealth War Graves Commission have listed him as killed in action on 29th April and it is probably correct.

Given the above it is no surprise to learn that Alfred has no known grave. But he is commemorated on the Menin Gate at Ypres, just one of nearly 55,000 *"missing"* men who lost their lives in the Ypres area during the Great War.

A photo of part of the panel with his name on is shown here.

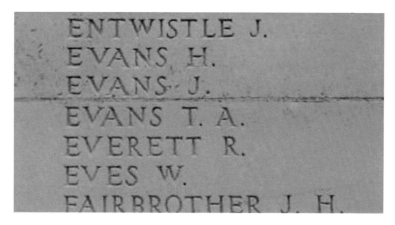

Alfred qualified for a British War Medal and Victory Medal and his parents would have received a Memorial Plaque and Scroll.

He is also commemorated on the Bromborough memorial in St. Barnabas's church, and on the Bromborough Pool Memorial (inside & outside St. Matthews church).

2ND. LIEUTENANT WILLIAM FITTON MM
Kings Liverpool Regt, Lancashire Fusiliers & 6th Squadron R.A.F.

WILLIAM FITTON WAS BORN TOWARDS the end of 1894, the son of William, a Farm Labourer, and Elizabeth (*"Bessie"*). The parents had married in 1888 at St. Andrew's church, Lower Bebington but were living in North Wales for a while after that. However by 1911 they were settled at No.262 New Chester Road, Port Sunlight (see photo) with their three surviving children. William was a member of the Port Sunlight Boys Brigade, while his father and older sister Elizabeth ("Lizzie") were working at Lever Brothers, with young Mary Louisa ("Louie") still at school. William was working as a Clerk at the Borough Treasurers, having finished his education at the prestigious Birkenhead Institute after winning a Levers scholarship from Port Sunlight school.

Wilfred Owen attended Birkenhead Institute from 1900-1907 so it is just possible that William, about 18 months younger than Owen, may have known him. After his death there were many family tributes paid to him in the local newspapers, and he was referred to as Billy - so from now on that is what he will be called here.

Billy started work as a Clerk for Birkenhead Corporation in August 1911 (aged 16) and was there for 3 years, before enlisting as 3061 Private Fitton in the 10th Battalion Kings Liverpool Regiment (Liverpool Scottish) on 5th August 1914.

He trained in the UK at King's Park, Edinburgh and at Tunbridge Wells before embarking on board the SS *"Maidan"* at Southampton on 1st November, arriving in France the same day.

He took part in the famous charge by the Liverpool Scottish at Hooge on June 16th 1915 when they were part of an attack on the German front line trenches near Bellewaarde Farm. They went over the top with 23 officers and 519 other ranks, and by the end of the day only 2 officers and 140 other ranks had escaped unscathed.

Final casualties for the days fighting included 6 Officers and well over 100 men killed. Happily, Billy was one of the men who escaped injury, and indeed a *"Birkenhead News"* report dated November 1916 confirmed that he had come through the war so far *"without a scratch"*.

Billy was awarded a Military Medal for his actions at Hooge on 16th May 1915. It seems that after the Battalion returned to camp a list of those men recommended for decoration or mention was prepared and sent to Brigade

Headquarters but it was destroyed in a fire. As a result no member of the Liverpool Scottish was decorated straight away. Three men did receive a Distinguished Conduct Medal on the recommendation of the Commanding Officers of other units, but in November 1916 ten men were eventually awarded a Military Medal in recognition of their conspicuous gallantry, and Billy was one of them. He was also promoted to Acting Sergeant at the same time.

He attended a 2nd Army course from 24th November 1916 to 26th January 1917 before being offered the chance of a commission on 10th March. He returned to the UK and attended an Officer Cadet Battalion at Gailes in Scotland which ultimately led to his commission as a 2nd Lieutenant in the 2nd Battalion of the Lancashire Fusiliers on 26th September 1917. However he wasn't with the Fusiliers for very long because he soon applied to join the Royal Flying Corps (later to become the Royal Air Force). He probably began training with them after 14th November when he passed his medical for work as a pilot. He spent some time training in the UK and it looks as though it was during this period that he got married.

It was 27th March 1918 at St. Catherine's church in Tranmere to be precise and his wife was Amy Naylor, the daughter of Alderman Fred Naylor J.P.

Amy worked for Lever Brothers in their Head Office in Port Sunlight. She had lost her younger brother Fred at Passchendaele about six months previously but little knew that her marriage was to last less than 5 months.

Billy finally arrived in France as a Pilot on 14th August, reaching his squadron on Sunday 18th. A picture of him in his RAF uniform is shown here.

He took his first flight in France the following evening and at a height of just 200 feet he got into a spin and crashed to the ground. It was thought that if the aircraft had been higher then he would have had a chance to manoeuvre to safety. He may not have died instantly though because his RAF service record states that he was admitted to hospital, but he certainly died the same evening aged just 23.

Billy is buried in Wavans British Cemetery, about 10 miles north west of Doullens. It is a very small cemetery with only 43 Commonwealth casualties, but 12 of them were in the RAF. The epitaph reads: *"Until We Meet"*

He is also commemorated on the Port Sunlight memorial, the Birkenhead Institute memorial, the Boys Brigade memorial in Christ Church, and on his parent's headstone in Bebington cemetery.

Apart from his Military Medal Billy also qualified for a 1914 Star, British War Medal & Victory Medal. His wife Amy would have received a Memorial Plaque and Scroll.

It is worth recording that his mother and father lived to ripe old ages – his father 97 and his mother 85. His young wife Amy died in Birkenhead in 1969 never having married again.

The author would like to thank the *"Liverpool Scottish Museum Trust"* for some of the information about Billy Fitton, particularly with regards to his Military Medal.

70249 PRIVATE HORACE HOLDEN
13th Battalion Royal Welsh Fusiliers

HORACE WAS BORN IN Port Sunlight on 30th July 1898 the son of Thomas & Elizabeth Holden (both originally from Penketh, near Warrington). Horace was one of eight surviving children on the 1911 census and in birth order they were Mary Ellen, Maggie, Thomas, Horace, Albert, Robert, Florence and Elizabeth.

The father Thomas was a Barge Master working for Lever Brothers, but he died in 1909 when Horace was just 10 years old.

In 1911 Elizabeth and her eight children were all living at No.16 Windy Bank in Port Sunlight village. A beautiful house, (pictured) but with just 4 rooms it must have been a tight squeeze for her big family. But at least the eldest three children were now all earning money – at Lever Brothers of course. They attended the Wesleyan church in Lower Bebington.

After his education at the village school Horace worked for Lever Brothers in No.2 Soap Room for a while, but later he joined Prices candle factory and he was there when war was declared.

He joined up with the Montgomeryshire Yeomanry in March 1917 aged 18, but he was transferred to the 13th Royal Welsh Fusiliers before being posted to France in September 1917.

The RWF Regimental Records mentions that on the 22nd April 1918 the 13th Battalion were near the Ancre valley. A *"minor"* attack on some higher ground was planned in order to secure better observation into the valley and the attack commenced just after 7am.

The position was eventually won, but at a huge cost. The battalion war diary reported :

"Exceedingly heavy machine gun fire was experienced immediately the attack commenced. Heavy casualties received. Hand to hand fighting took place in which much bayoneting was done and severe casualties inflicted on enemy. ------- *Our casualties heavy. Machine gun fire active all night"*

Casualties for the day were reported in the regimental records as 6 officers and 62 other ranks killed, with 3 officers and 201 other ranks wounded.

Horace was one of these 201, with wounds to his hip and arm. He was invalided back to the UK ending up in an Aberdeen hospital.

His chances looked quite good at first, but after being in hospital for several weeks he died suddenly on the 26th June, aged 19.

His body was returned to Port Sunlight and the funeral was held on Saturday June 29th with full military honours. He is buried in a family grave in Christ Church (see photo).

Horace qualified for a British War Medal and Victory Medal and his widowed mother would also have received a Memorial Plaque and Scroll.

He is also commemorated on the Port Sunlight memorial, the Wesleyan memorial in Lower Bebington and the Bromborough Pool memorial (inside & outside St. Matthew's church).

10695 PRIVATE JAMES GRIFFITHS
8th Battalion - Cheshire Regiment

JAMES GRIFFITHS WAS BORN IN Higher Bebington in 1892. He probably lived in Mount Road at first, with his parents James (a Labourer) and Sarah Ann (nee Johnson) who had married in Liverpool in 1885.

His father died in 1895 aged just 47 and his mother remarried in 1898 to Ralph Wright. They were living at 4 Prospect Hill in 1901 and his stepfather worked as a Farm Labourer.

In 1911 his mother & step father were living at Storeton Hall Cottages, probably provided through Ralph's work on the farm there. James had flown the nest by this time, and to be perfectly honest he seems to have disappeared off the face of the earth! He didn't marry so his whereabouts in 1911 is a mystery.

He had 3 sisters from his mother's first marriage, Elizabeth, Bessie and Sarah Ann and his half brothers and sisters were Hannah, George Henry, and Mary.

In a letter sent home to his mother from training camp in Pirbright he signed off with *"from your son Jim"* so that is what he will be known as here too.

His army service record has not survived, but his medal card has.

However it is known that Jim enlisted with the 8th Battalion Cheshire Regiment on the 11th August 1914 and undertook his training in Tidworth, Chiseldon, and finally at Pirbright Camp, Surrey. He was trained as a Signaller.

The Battalion left the UK in June 1915 and disembarked in Egypt on 26th June en route for Gallipoli. The *"Birkenhead News"* reported that he had landed at Gallipoli under heavy shell fire on 14th July and was fighting more or less continuously until 27th October when he was hit and killed by a shell near Chocolate Hill.

An exact transcription of the Battalion war diary follows :-

25th - Weather fine and calm, getting warmer. Enemy shelled reserve trenches 3 casualties.

26th – 2nd Lt. G.S. Sheard went to hospital. Strong southerly wind. Weather warmer.

27th – 9.00 - 9.45 am - Enemy shelled reserve trenches. 2 casualties, 1 killed and 1 wounded.

11.45 – 12 noon – Bombardment of all trenches by enemy using battery fire. No casualties. The bombardment included the lines of 38th Brigade on our right on Chocolate Hill.

It is safe to assume that Jim was the man killed between 9.00 & 9.45am

He died aged 23, and is buried in Green Hill Cemetery. The ground conditions here make it too difficult to erect standard headstones so most of the graves are marked with a stone *"box"* – see photo. There are nearly 3,000 servicemen buried or commemorated in this cemetery, but sadly most are unidentified.

Jim was awarded a 1915 Star, British War Medal and Victory Medal and his mother Sarah would have received a memorial Plaque and Scroll.

He is the same James Griffiths that is also on the Christ Church memorial in Higher Bebington, and he may also be commemorated on the Birkenhead War Memorial.

Although no direct link for Jim can be made with Lower Bebington, it is felt certain that this is the correct man named on the memorial. Next of kin data for St. Andrew's memorial compiled in the early 1920's confirms that James Griffiths' name was supplied by a visitor from Storeton (see extract below).

Name supplied by one of Storeton District Visor will try to supply address later.

LIEUTENANT KENNETH GEORGE HASLAM FORD
11th Cheshire Regiment

KENNETH WAS BORN ON 12TH November 1895. His father George Adam Ford was born in Macclesfield but spent his formative years in Liverpool, being a teacher of Classics & Mathematics in 1881. He later became Senior Chaplain to Her Majesty's Indian Ecclesiastical Establishment and was the Archdeacon and Commissary of Lucknow. He was missing from the censuses of 1891 & 1901 and so it is likely that he was in India during those years.

At the time of the Great War he was the Rector of Bebington – and there lies Kenneth's link to the town.

Kenneth's mother was Ellen Isabella Barrett, the daughter of Rev. Canon J.M. Barrett. She may have married George in India about 1890, but Kenneth was born at St. Margaret's Vicarage, Lincoln – Ellen's parent's home.

It is doubtful whether Kenneth spent much time in India, because he was educated at South Lodge School, Lowestoft and later at

Marlborough College. During his time at Marlborough Kenneth spent 4 years in the Officers Training Corps. He continued this in 1913, being a Private in the Inns of Court O.T.C.

The 1911 census reveals that the parents had a total of seven children, but only four were still surviving. In birth order they were : Kenneth, Patricia Margaret, Bridget Audrey and Terence Gilbert. They had not yet arrived at Bebington though, the address given was No.8 Adamson Road, London and Kenneth was on the census for Marlborough College.

On the very day Britain declared war on Germany, 4th August 1914, Kenneth presented himself at a recruiting office in Bristol and enlisted as No.1411 in the 1st South Midlands Brigade of the Royal Field Artillery. He was working in Bristol as an *"Engineers pupil"* at Messrs. Humpage, Thompson and Hardy – machine tool makers, listing his age as 18 years 9 months and with his parents living at the Rectory in Bebington (so they had finally arrived in Bebington).

His army medical reveals that he was very tall, 6'-2" yet only 10 stone.

He had not been in the Artillery for very long before he was offered a commission in the 11th Battalion of the Cheshire Regiment.

His father had written a letter to the Secretary of State pleading for his son to be considered for this and it seemed to pay swift dividends when he was transferred to the 11th Cheshires as a 2nd Lieutenant on 22nd September. This was followed up by promotion to Lieutenant on 24th November, and at the same time he was appointed as commanding officer of the Battalion's machine gun section.

They trained at Codford St. Mary, Bournemouth and Aldershot before being posted to France, arriving there on 25th September 1915.

At the end of November 1915 the Battalion were at Ploegsteert Wood, about 8 miles south of Ypres in Belgium, and the war diary reported that they were close to a position popularly known as the Birdcage.

On the 30th the enemy were more active than usual in the morning, and the war diary account of what happened next is given here: *"12.45pm - Lieutenant Ford, machine gun officer, whilst observing at the Picket House was severely wounded in the head by an enemy sniper, who put three shots in quick succession through a loophole in the trench wall. Lieut. Ford was hit by the first shot. He was conveyed by all possible speed to Bailleul hospital but unfortunately succumbed to his wound during the night".*

Officially he died the following day, 1st December so he probably died in the early hours. He had only just turned 19.

Naturally, his parents received many tributes to their son, but the one from Captain Graham Satow, the Brigade Machine Gun Officer told a little more of what had happened : *"He was the keenest Machine Gun Officer in the Brigade, and indeed, his keenness has lost us his services for ever. He was conducting a reconnaissance in the front line of our trenches, trying to locate a German emplacement. He died through carrying out a dangerous duty, like the fearless lad he was. All honour to you and him for it."*

A memorial service for him was held at St.Andrew's church on Wednesday afternoon the 8th December 1915.

In 1917 his father asked for permission to erect a memorial for him in the church itself, and being the Rector of the Parish, it could hardly be refused!

It is still there today of course, and takes the form of a marble tablet and a restored statue of St.Andrew. A photograph of the tablet is shown here.

Kenneth is buried in Bailleul Communal Cemetery Extension, which contains over 4,400 Commonwealth casualties from the Great War.
   The epitaph, chosen (and paid for) by his parents reads :

"Machine Gun Officer
Faithful Unto Death
A Dieu and Au Revoir"

He qualified for a 1915 Star, British War Medal and Victory Medal and his parents received a Memorial Plaque and Scroll.
   By the end of the war, his parents had moved to *"The Rectory"* Ashill, Norfolk.

1604 GUNNER THOMAS HOUGHTON GATES

"C" Battery : 277th Brigade : Royal Field Artillery

THOMAS WAS BORN IN LIVERPOOL during the first few months of 1875. He was one of at least five children born to Levi Gates and his wife Eliza (nee Houghton), who were both from Budworth in Cheshire originally. The couple had married at St. Luke's church in Liverpool in 1862 but from the time of the 1881 census to 1911 their address was No.12 York Street in Bromborough Pool. Levi had been working for Price's Candles all these years, as Captain of a steam barge.

The children in birth order were : James, Charles, Thomas Houghton, Harry, and Bessie.

Sadly Eliza died in 1903, but Levi carried on at York Street and in 1911 he had his son Harry's family living with him.

Thomas, meanwhile, had married Sophia Roberts at St. Andrew's in 1902 and by 1911 they were living at 54 Trafalgar Drive, Lower Bebington (see photo) with their daughter Sophia.

Thomas was employed as a Cooper, as he had been since 1891, and he must have been working at Price's Candles like his father because he is named on the Bromborough Pool factory memorial.

His army service papers have survived, and provide us with some useful information.

He attested at Liverpool on 9th January 1915 as 1604 Gunner Thomas Gates, in the 3rd West Lancashire Brigade, Royal Field Artillery.

His medical reveals that he was 5'-9" tall, and weighed 10 stone. Curiously he had a toe missing from his left foot!

The Brigade trained in the UK before being posted overseas, arriving in France on 1st October 1915.

Little more is known about Thomas' service other than that he was killed in action on 31st August 1916, aged 41. The Battery were at a place referred to in the war diary as Brick Point, almost a mile south of Montauban, and they had been shelling German positions at Guillemont for four days. On the morning of 31st at 9.15am they were heavily shelled with Lachrymatory gas, 3 men were killed and their positions much damaged. The enemy shelling continued for 19 hours. One section was relieved at 9am and the other at 4pm. There was great difficulty in carrying out the relief due to the gas hanging in the valley and dug-outs.

Thomas was one of the 3 men killed on that day.

He is buried in Flatiron Copse Cemetery, Mametz, and a photograph of his headstone is shown.
Over 1,500 Commonwealth casualties are buried here.

Thomas qualified for a 1915 Star, British War Medal, and Victory Medal. His wife Sophia would also have received a Memorial Plaque and Scroll.

He is also commemorated on the Bromborough Pool memorial, both inside and outside St. Matthews church, and on the West Lancs Brigade memorial at Garston British Legion.

HIS WIFE SOPHIA WAS AWARDED a pension for herself and their only child, but not payable until 19th March 1917.

Shortly after the war she was living at *"Ashbyrne"*, Cross Lane, Bebington.

Lower Bebington Gunner Killed.

Mrs. Gates, of 54 Trafalgar-drive, Lower Bebington, has received word that her husband, Gunner Thomas Houghton Gates, was killed in action on August 31st. He was 41 years of age and in the R.F.A.

49099 PRIVATE HERBERT ALLAN BROWN
17th Battalion – Kings Liverpool Regiment

HERBERT WAS A TWIN SON of George Herbert Allan Brown and Alice Brown (nee Little). Curiously, on the censuses from 1891 to 1911 the father was listed as either born *"at sea"* or in Calcutta. He was an artist, painting pottery at least some of the time, Alice was also born abroad, in Auckland, New Zealand.

However, they had married locally, at West Derby in Liverpool in 1885 and soon after they set up home in Sidney Road, Lower Tranmere. The twins Herbert and George arrived on 22nd November 1886, followed later by Harold, Alice and Hilda. Alice died at the age of 9, but like most of the children she had the middle name of Allan.

By 1901 the family had moved to No.12 Trafalgar Drive and moved further up the road to No.46 in 1911 (see photo).

Herbert was working as a Clerk in a sawmill at the age of 24, while his twin brother was following in his fathers footsteps, being listed as a student of sculpture on the 1911 census.

It can be assumed that the family attended the nearby St. Andrews church because Herbert sang in the church choir for many years. Indeed, after his death in the war a beautiful plaque was put up in his memory inside the church (see photo.)

The plaque incorrectly mentions the 13th Cheshires, but Herbert was definitely with the 17th Kings Liverpool when he was killed.

Herberts army papers have not survived so very little can be discovered about his enlistment. He originally signed up as (Private) 4601 for the Cheshires but at some point transferred to the 17th Kings Liverpools.

He wasn't posted overseas until 11th October 1916 and arrived with the 17th Battalion on the 22nd serving with "A" company.

He was guilty of a misdemeanour after this, being awarded 7 days field punishment No.1 for urinating in a trench - we have all been desperate I am sure!

He suffered with Myalgia on 3rd April 1917 and received hospital treatment, not rejoining his Battalion until 8th May 1917.

Just a month later on 8th June 1917 he was reported *"missing believed killed"*

The war diary briefly reported that the Battalion were in trenches between Poperinghe and Abele in Belgium on 8th & 9th. Casualties for the two days were given as 4 men killed and 15 wounded.

It was confirmed that Herbert was one of the 4 men killed, aged 30.
Unfortunately his body was never recovered and so he is listed on the
Menin Gate in Ypres as one of those with no known grave.

Herbert was awarded a British War Medal and Victory Medal, and his
parents would also have received a Memorial Plaque and Scroll.
   His twin brother George seems to have avoided the war completely,
nothing could be found for him.

R38396 PRIVATE GEORGE WHITEHEAD
8th Battalion - Kings Royal Rifle Corps

GEORGE'S PARENTS WERE ORIGINALLY FROM the Neston/Thornton Hough area, and his father John David Whitehead had married Sarah Ellen Parry at All Saints church in Thornton Hough in 1898. They had moved to 87 Greendale Road by 1901 and John was working as a General Labourer at Lever Brothers.

Young George was the first of their 3 children listed on the 1911 census, but it is likely that they had another 3 children after this.

George himself was born in Thornton Hough in 1899, and his two brothers Wilfred and John arrived soon after the family had moved to Port Sunlight. They were still living at the same address, almost opposite the train station, in 1911.

George would have attended the village school and then, as was usual with this family orientated business, he was offered a job at Lever Brothers.

Given George's young age he would not have been required for training by the army until at least 1916 so he carried on working at the soap works in No.2 Woodbox.

Unfortunately there are no service records available for George, but when the time did come for him to join up it would probably have been with a Training Reserve Battalion, and at the time he was posted overseas he may well have been allocated to a regiment in need of reinforcements. In his case it was the 8th Battalion of the Kings Royal Rifle Corps, and with no army records or newspaper reports available we cannot be certain when he did eventually arrive in France.

It is quite likely that he had not been at the front very long before he was killed, but all we can be sure of is that George died of wounds on 4th April 1918 aged just 19.

The German Spring Offensive had started on 21st March and the Battalion were just a small part of the 41st Brigade in the 14th Division. The Division had suffered almost 6,000 casualties since the offensive had begun and according to the Battalion war diary by 1st April the 8th Kings Royal Rifles were down to a strength of just 3 officers and 80 other ranks. It appears from the scanty information given in the war diary at this chaotic time that the Battalion had a lot of men taken prisoner at the start of the offensive.

On the 4th April the war diary reported that they were in a support position at Bois-de-Vaire, and at 4am they received a warning of an impending German attack. Soon after this they suffered heavy shelling for 4 hours but had very few casualties. By 10am though, after severe fighting and being greatly outnumbered, they were in danger of being overrun and were forced to withdraw. In the evening they moved again to a support line in front of Aubigne. At this point the Battalion consisted of just 2 officers and 43 other ranks.

Because George died of wounds he may have received his injuries in the previous couple of days, but he is buried nearby at Villers-Bretonneux Military Cemetery near Aubigne.

This cemetery contains over 2,000 Commonwealth casualties from the Great War, and a photo of George's headstone is shown here.

He qualified for a British War Medal and Victory Medal, and his parents would have received a Memorial Plaque and Scroll.

George is also commemorated on the Port Sunlight memorial.

5TH ENGINEER OFFICER HARRY GEORGE
Mercantile Marine

HARRY WAS BORN ON 7TH July 1895 the son of Edward and Louisa George. The parents started off married life in New Ferry but moved to Bromborough Pool about 1900, living at 33 South View, Bromborough Pool for many years. Edward was employed as a Joiner at Prices candle works.

On the 1911 census there were seven surviving children, in order of birth these were Florence, Thomas, Louisa, Harry, Samuel, Robert Russell and Annie Kathleen. Harry and two of his siblings were also working at the candle works by now, Harry as a wood box maker although he later worked in the Fitters shop.

It is not clear when Harry joined the Mercantile Marine, but his work in the Fitters shop at Prices probably paved the way for him to eventually become a junior Engineer Officer on *"H.M.T. Eloby"*.

The Eloby was a 6,545 ton Elder Dempster ship, only built in 1913 but probably commandeered by the Navy for the duration of the war. She was lightly armed and was to be used as a transport or troop ship.

On 19th July 1917 she was reported to be carrying 56 crew, 100 French artillery troops, and some mules. The Eloby was about 75 miles south east of Malta when the German submarine U.38 torpedoed her without warning. There were no survivors, and Harry was drowned at the age of just 22.

Harry lived just 4 doors away from Roland Green, whose story is told elsewhere in this book.

His brothers Thomas and Robert also joined up and, just like Harry, their names are commemorated on the village memorial to all those who served. This is outside the now defunct St. Matthew's church in the village. Inside the church is a beautiful stone tablet with just the names of the fallen on it, and Harry is of course named on this as well.

The casualties of the *"Eloby"* are all named on the Tower Hill memorial in London, which contains the names of about 36,000 sailors whose bodies were never recovered.

The photograph clearly shows the name *"Eloby"* at top left with what is a long list of names – with *"George H."* near the bottom left.

Harry's parents would have been entitled to claim his British War Medal and a Mercantile Marine War Medal (below)

12692 PRIVATE JOSEPH WILLIAM DUTTON
9th Battalion Cheshire Regiment

JOSEPH WAS BORN IN BEBINGTON on 30th July 1895, the youngest of four children to Joseph & Elizabeth Dutton, both from the Malpas area of Cheshire originally. According to the census the father seems to have been working as a *"Car Proprietor"* – perhaps a Chauffeur?

The parents had been living in Bebington from about 1880 and all of their four children were born here – George, Kate, Elsie and Joseph. In 1901 the family were living at No.20 The Village, and there was an Elizabeth Harrison living next door at No.22.

Sadly, both parents seem to have died while Joseph was young. Joseph senior in 1903 and Elizabeth in 1907, but happily for Joseph he was taken in by Elizabeth Harrison at No.22, being listed as a Boarder on the 1911 census. He was just 15 and working as a General Labourer at Lever Brothers. His two sisters were now working as *"live in"* servants.

JOSEPH ENLISTED WITH THE CHESHIRES at Birkenhead on 1st September 1914. His service record tells us that he was C of E, 5'-6½" tall, just under 9 stone, with a pale complexion, fair hair and hazel eyes. After his training in Basingstoke and Salisbury Plain he was posted to France, landing at Boulogne on 19th July 1915.

It was reported that he suffered with scabies in January 1916 and needed treatment for a month, and apart from a minor misdemeanour there was nothing else to report until his death on the night of 16th/17th July 1917, aged 21.

The 9th Battalion were at Onraete Wood near Wytschaete, a few miles south of Ypres and the war diary does not report anything untoward occurring that night. Joseph was the orderly of Lt. Aubrey Gallie, and in a letter to Joseph's sister the officer wrote :

"I cannot find words to express my sympathy to you in the loss of your dear brother. He was, I am sorry to say killed on the night of the 17th. It was instantaneous and he suffered absolutely no pain. He was my orderly. I was standing not many yards away from him when it happened. - - - - -"

Officially he is simply recorded as killed in action, and so we can only guess that it could have been a sniper that got him?

His sister, who was married in 1914 and was now Kate Norris living in Bromborough, had been in regular contact with Joseph. She had received a letter from him on 10th July letting her know that he would be home on leave in August.

Joseph is buried close to where he was killed, in Oosttaverne Wood cemetery.

The epitaph (chosen by his sister) is :

"He died that we might live"

There are over 440 Commonwealth casualties in this cemetery, some of them from World War 2.

Joseph qualified for a 1915 Star, British War Medal, and Victory Medal. His sister should have received these, along with a Memorial Plaque and Scroll.

He is also commemorated on the Port Sunlight Memorial.

THE FIRST DAY OF THE SOMME

MOST PEOPLE SEEM TO BE aware of this day, even if they have no interest at all in the Great War, but the following few paragraphs are written for those who don't know much of what happened.

In order to relieve enormous German pressure on the French further south, at Verdun in particular, it had been agreed by the British that they would launch a major attack in the summer of 1916 on the German line either side of the River Somme. After a colossal week long artillery bombardment of the German trenches the British Army went over the top at 7.30am on 1st July 1916, only to find that their barrage had failed to damage the German barbed wire or their huge underground bunkers. In most places on the front as soon as the bombardment ceased German machine gunners emerged from their dug outs and mowed down the advancing British infantry.

It was, and still is, the worst day in the history of the British army. Losses were fifteen times worse than on D-Day in 1944.

Overall British casualties on the first day can vary depending on what books you read, but in Martin Middlebrook's *"The First Day on the Somme"* he gives the following figures as a final return :

Killed or Died of Wounds (all ranks)	19,240	
Wounded (all ranks)	35,493	
Missing (all ranks)	2,152	
Taken Prisoner (all ranks)	585	Total 57,470

The idea of Pals Battalions fell out of favour after the 1st July. There were entire streets in many smaller towns receiving telegrams with the bad news. As an example the 11th Battalion East Lancashire Regiment (the Accrington Pals) attacked at Serre and of the 720 men who took part in the attack 584 were killed, wounded or missing.

The following few pages will tell the stories of three of the four Bebington men who were killed or fatally wounded on that awful day. The other man, Frank Davies, is to be found at the start of the book – he was the second of the four Davies brothers who died in the war.

L/9578 SERGEANT FREDERICK DELLOW
2nd & 4th Battalions Middlesex Regiment

USING THE POPULAR DEFINITION OF the term, Frederick Dellow was a Cockney because he was born in Bow, London in 1885 (presumably within the sound of the bells).

His father John Samuel Dellow had died not long after Frederick was born and on the 1891 census his widowed mother Mary Ann was living in Mile End, Old Town, London and supporting her children by working as a corset maker. The children (in birth order) were John, Mary, Charles, Joseph, Edith, Cecilia, and Frederick. In 1901 four of the children (including Frederick) were still at home and living in Hackney.

In January 1904 at the age of 18 years & 5 months Frederick joined the 4th Battalion of the Middlesex Regiment. At the age of 18 he was 5'-6" tall, 8½ stone, with hazel eyes and light brown hair. He was also C. of E.

HE HAD LISTED HIS PREVIOUS trade as a Wood Japanner but just a year later he was serving with the *"Die Hards"*as they liked to be known in the Transvaal, South Africa. He travelled the world with the Middlesex, later serving in China, Singapore and India. He was overseas for about 7 years and there a few misdemeanours along the way – including gambling, drunkenness, neglect of duty, but the army still seemed to think very well of him because he reached the rank of Lance Sergeant.

He finally returned to the UK from Bombay in October 1911.

In 1912 he was actually court martialled. It seems that on 6th June he left parade in Devonport and went absent without leave for two days.

According to Frederick's own defence *"I remember coming off parade after drilling recruits. After that I cannot remember anything until I found myself at Bournemouth, where I gave myself up to a policeman on 8th June."*

A witness spoke up for Frederick at the court martial, and mention was also made of a case of sunstroke he had suffered in Singapore a year or so before.

Unfortunately his service record does not make it clear what the outcome of the court martial was, but he remained in the army until August 1913 when he was placed on the army reserve (with his own consent) five months short of his 10 years service.

By now the reader may have formed the impression that Frederick Dellow was a very colourful character, and may also be wondering why a cockney is commemorated on the St. Andrews memorial.

The answer to the second point seems to lie with his older sister Edith who had been listed on the 1901 census as a cardboard box maker (in London). But on the 1911 census she was a 30 year old Forewoman in the fancy card box department at Lever Brothers. She was living in a company house with her mother and two boarders, at No.42 Park Road. Curiously the two female boarders (sisters) were both born in St. Pancras, London and were also working at Levers.

With Frederick's sister and mother having been settled in Port Sunlight for a few years, and him leaving the army in 1913, it can be safely assumed that he had been up to visit them. And sure enough he found himself a job as a Gateman at the soap factory, and on 20th December 1913 he also married a local girl Sarah Bennett at St. Andrews. The newly married couple soon started a family with a daughter Mabel being born on 29th September the following year. Sadly it was to be their only child, because the war intervened.

With Frederick still being on the army reserve he was mobilised immediately on 5th August 1914 and given the rank of Sergeant – so there was obviously no hard feelings about the court martial! He also retained the 9578 number he was given in 1904 but with a prefix of "L" it is believed that this was to signify that he had been a pre-war regular. At this point Frederick and his wife were living at Erfurt Avenue (at the back of St. Andrews churchyard) although at the time of his death in 1916 his wife was living at No.13 Heath Road.

Frederick was with the 2nd Battalion and although they landed at Le Havre on 7th November for some reason he didn't get posted overseas until 4th January 1915. It wasn't too long before the Battalion were in serious action at the Battle of Neuve Chapelle.

Frederick wrote an account of the fighting in a letter he sent home to Lever Brothers.

On 9th March the 2nd Battalion left their barracks and took up position for an attack the following morning.

They went over the top at about 8am on 10th but got held up by the German barbed wire which had not been damaged by the British artillery bombardment. Two German machine guns inflicted heavy casualties and the "Die Hards" were forced to retire three times. By midday, at the fourth attempt, they succeeded in getting through the wire and into the German trenches.

Sgt. Dellow was confronted by a German, both of them had bayonets at the ready but before either of them could move the German took a bullet in the side and collapsed. Frederick said he saw the mans face for days afterwards.

The Battalion were in reserve the following day and had entrenched themselves in an orchard but still took casualties from heavy shelling, some men were buried alive or blown into the trees by the explosions.

On 12th they fought off a German counter attack, inflicting heavy casualties on them in the process, Frederick wrote that they had fallen in their hundreds.

At 9pm on the 13th they took up position in a fire trench and the following morning Frederick reported that there were dead men everywhere you looked. He walked along the trench and there were brave men weeping, Frederick was also badly affected but one of the men had started playing *"Get out and get under"* on his mouth organ and it lifted everyone's spirits.

They spent the rest of the day repairing their trench and that night they were relieved, and what was left of them marched to billets 3 miles behind the line.

Frederick said that they looked a right mess, with clothes torn and nearly all covered in blood.

As a reflection on the severity of the fighting, the official war diary gave casualty figures for the period 10th – 14th March as 7 officers killed and 8 wounded with 70 other ranks killed, 299 wounded, and 89 missing. These were numbers arrived at in the immediate aftermath, and Soldiers Died in the Great War actually gives 146 other ranks killed. This far greater number will be because many of the missing were later confirmed as dead.

A COUPLE OF WEEKS LATER on 31st March the Battalion were in trenches between St. Eloi and Armentieres and during the afternoon a shell burst in the trench. Frederick was slightly wounded in the left leg and he was waiting for darkness to fall before going to the dressing station to get it looked at when a spent bullet hit his left hand, fracturing his second finger. These were what were popularly known as *"Blighty"* wounds, bad enough to get you home for treatment and recuperation and it must have been at this point that Frederick had the photograph on the previous page taken.

THE WOUNDS CLEARED UP WITHOUT too much trouble, and the lady commandant of the Sussex hospital that treated his wounds commented that the staff were all much attached to him especially for his *"brightness and good influence."*

After his recuperation he returned to the front (probably on May 15th) but this time he was posted to the 4th Battalion.

Frederick had no further mishaps in 1915 and he also made it through safely to the notorious opening day of the Battle of the Somme on 1st July 1916.

The 4th Middlesex were just in front of Fricourt (about 3 miles due east of Albert) and they were part of the 63rd Brigade in the 21st Division. The plan was for them to go over the top and attack the German trenches at 7.25 am and an intense preliminary bombardment of the German positions had started an hour before this. (In fact the British had been bombarding the German trenches for 8 days). The German artillery had retaliated and caused considerable casualties in the Middlesex front line trench, particularly to *"A"* company.

The following is a transcript from the Battalion war diary which graphically describes the days desperate fighting :

"The leading platoons attempted to leave the trenches at 7:25am in accordance with instructions, but suffered severely from most terrific machine gun fire and had to get back. Two mines were exploded at 7.28 am on our right near the German Tambour. The leading platoons left the trenches again, slightly before 7:30 am, the actual hour of assault, and were met by intense rifle and machine gun fire. The remainder of

"A" & "B" companies followed in lines of platoons at 100 yard distance. "C" company followed them in two lines, two platoons in each line, at the same distance. "D" company in the same formation came last, the rear line carrying the Battalion reserve of ammunition and grenades. Battalion headquarters moved with the rear line of "C" company. The leading boys, reached and passed over the German front line. By this time all the officers, with the exception of Lieut. Simpson, and most of the non commissioned officers had been hit. The survivors pushed on most gallantly, in small groups, beyond the support line. Between this line and the sunken road, in spite of most severe hand to hand fighting, (in which butts of rifles & bayonets, & even fists were used) and heavy losses, they were unable to maintain themselves, until the arrival of the supporting Battalions. The remnants of the Battalion attached themselves to the 8th Lincoln Regiment on their arrival and remained with them until the morning of 3rd July when they were brought back to Battalion headquarters by Sergt. Millwood."

They were not finally relieved until 3am on the 4th July when they marched back to Dernancourt.

The 1st July was the blackest day ever for the British army, with over 19,000 men killed on this one day.

The 4th Battalion Middlesex casualties (all ranks) from 1st – 3rd July are given in the war diary as 186 killed, 341 wounded, 15 missing believed killed, and 38 missing. Some of the wounded would have died several days later (as Frederick did).

Frederick received his fatal wounds on the 1st July. He was removed to a casualty clearing station several miles behind the lines where he eventually died a week later on July 7th probably at the age of 30 or 31, although his headstone says 29.

He is buried in Heilly Station Cemetery, Mericourt-L'Abbe.

There are nearly 3,000 Commonwealth servicemen in this cemetery, but due to the extreme pressure on burials at this time many of them are very close together, and also 2 or 3 to a grave.

As can be seen from the photo of Frederick's headstone. Private J. Hughes of the Royal Fusiliers is buried with him.

The epitaph for Frederick, chosen by his wife, reads: *"While Christ the Spirit keepeth the wearied frame hath rest".*

Frederick qualified for the 1915 Star, British War Medal, and Victory Medal. His wife would have received a Memorial Plaque and Scroll. He is also commemorated on the Port Sunlight Memorial.

His papers reveal that his widow Sarah was awarded 16 shillings a week pension for her and their daughter.

16244 LANCE SERGEANT HENRY VICTOR HUGHES
18th Battalion - Kings Liverpool Regiment

HENRY WAS BORN IN LIVERPOOL on 8th July 1887. He was the son of John Lister Hughes, a Pawnbroker, and his wife Eleanor (nee Fey). The parents were Liverpudlians and they were to have 8 children, all born in the city between 1878 and 1893. In birth order they were : Richard Ellis, Louisa Margaret, John Fey, Eleanor Lister, Hartley Gordon, Henry Victor, Edith Harrington, and Olive Jessie. The family were living in Breck Road, Anfield in 1891 and the Pawnbroking business must have been doing well because they could afford to employ a servant. By 1901 though they had moved to No.306 New Chester Road, Port Sunlight and John was working at Lever Brothers. Henry had joined the Church Lads Brigade while still at school, and later played Rugby Union for the Cosmopolitans club.

His father died in 1906 aged 62, at which point Henry was 18. On the 1911 census Eleanor and six of the children were living just down the road at No.278 New Chester Road. This was a company house with a magnificent chimney stack (see photo), and although John had died no less than five of the children were employed in the soap works.

Henry had completed his education at the prestigious Birkenhead Institute, most probably having gained a scholarship from Lever Brothers. Sometime after his schooling he started work as a Commercial Clerk at Levers in 1908, and remained there until the war started, by which time he was just turned 27.

He attested to the 18th Battalion of the Kings Liverpool Regiment in Liverpool on 3rd September 1914 (the day after Percy Parry). His medical revealed what a big man he was. 6'-1¾" tall, just over 11 stone, with fresh complexion, grey eyes, and brown hair. He was also Church of England.

The 18th Battalion were the 2nd City Battalion, or more popularly the 2nd Liverpool Pals and during their period of training in the UK Henry was promoted to Lance Corporal (on 7th October 1914). Just a couple of weeks or so later he became a Corporal, and then again on 27th March 1915 he was promoted, this time to Lance Sergeant.

They were posted overseas on 6th November 1915, embarking on board the S.S. *"Invicta"* and they arrived in Boulogne the following day. It is interesting to note that at least three Port Sunlight men were amongst them (John Lewis and Percy Parry's stories are also told elsewhere in this book).

Henry was escaping any serious injury, just suffering a badly sprained ankle on 29th March 1916. After recuperation he was back on duty by 22nd April.

His service record notes that he was promoted to Sergeant on 10th June, but perhaps because he was killed just 3 weeks later this promotion was never confirmed. He is recorded only as a Lance Sergeant on official records.

Henry aged 28, and Percy Parry, were both killed in action on the 1st July 1916, the infamous first day of the Battle of the Somme. This is written about a little earlier in the book because four Bebington men were either killed or fatally wounded on this day.

The Pals were a part of 30th Division, and the Divisions objective on the first day was to take the village of Montauban. Using the Battalion war diary the basic facts are as follows :

The 18th Kings were ordered to be in their assembly trenches in Talus Boise (just south of Montauban) by midnight on the 30th June. They were to be fully equipped and ready for the big attack.

At 6.30am the British artillery started an intensive bombardment of the German trenches, and at 7.30 am the Battalion left their own trenches. Their attack was pressed home with great spirit and determination in spite of heavy shelling and machine gun enfilade fire which caused casualties amounting to about 2/3 of the Battalion strength. They had captured Montauban by 11am and the whole system of German trenches including the Glatz Redoubt were also captured without any deviation from the scheduled programme.

Having achieved their objectives they consolidated their position and made strong points as a defence against any possible counter attacks.

This was one of the rare successes on the 1st July, but it was at a terrible cost. Soldiers Died in the Great War gives the awful figures :
6 Officers and 160 Other Ranks killed in action. Total casualties including wounded were estimated at 500. Some of these men would die of wounds in the days or weeks ahead. Over 30 of the dead had Wirral connections.

It was reported that Henry was leading his Platoon in the big attack when he was struck down by a bullet and killed. An officer wrote to his mother and included the comment *"- - - he was one of those men who did his duty all the better the more danger there was."*

Henry has no known grave, but he is commemorated on the Thiepval memorial. This huge memorial lists the names of over 72,000 men who died at the Somme, but whose bodies were never found.

He qualified for a 1915 Star, British War Medal and Victory Medal.

Never having married, Henry's mother Eleanor would also have received a Memorial Plaque and Scroll.

Henry is also commemorated on the Port Sunlight memorial and on the Birkenhead Institute memorial (nowadays housed in Birkenhead Central Library).

Henry's older brother Hartley Gordon Hughes (a Schoolteacher) appears to have served in the war, in the Royal Garrison Artillery. Happily he survived.

16198 PRIVATE HERBERT PERCY PARRY
18th Battalion - Kings Liverpool Regiment

HE SEEMS TO HAVE BEEN known as Percy, and he is actually named on the St.Andrews memorial as *"H. Percy Parry."*

Percy was born on the 29th April 1894 in Liverpool, one of five children born to William and Jane Parry (nee Bayley) both parents were from Liverpool. On the 1901 census the family were living at Barrington Road in the Toxteth Park area of the city, but William was working as a Book Keeper for Lever Brothers.

By 1911 they had moved to Port Sunlight and were living at No.9 Riverside (see photo) and the father was still working as a Book Keeper.

The children, in birth order were : William, Arthur Edward, Amy Mildred, Alfred Francis, and Herbert Percy.

Percy was now 16 and working as a Clerk for a Steamship Company. However he started work in the Cash Office at Levers soon after and he was still there when war was declared.

161

Just like Henry Hughes and John Lewis he chose to enlist with the 18th Battalion of the Kings Liverpool Regiment (2nd Liverpool Pals). In fact all three of them signed up on 2nd or 3rd September 1914 - Percy on the 2nd.

His army medical reveals that he was

5'-6" tall, just 8 stone in weight, with grey eyes, light brown hair and a sallow complexion. He was also C.of E.

The Battalion were posted overseas on 6th November 1915 embarking on board the S.S. *"Invicta"* and they arrived in Boulogne the following day.

According to his service record nothing untoward occurred to Percy from 7th November 1915 when he arrived in France, until 1st July 1916 – the first day of the Somme.

Percy's story on this fateful day is very similar to Henry Hughes' but it will be detailed again here nevertheless.

The 18th Kings were ordered to be in their assembly trenches in Talus Boise (just south of Montauban) by midnight on the 30th June. They were to be fully equipped and ready for the big attack.

At 6.30am the British artillery started an intensive bombardment of the German trenches. And at 7.30 am the Battalion left their own trenches, the attack was pressed home with great spirit and determination in spite of heavy shelling and machine gun enfilade fire which caused casualties amounting to about 2/3 of the Battalion strength. They captured Montauban by 11am and also the whole system of German trenches including the Glatz Redoubt were captured without any deviation from the scheduled programme.

Having achieved their objectives they consolidated their position and made strong points as a defence against any possible counter attacks.

At some point on this day (probably before 11am) Percy was killed in action at the age of 22.

At first he was just reported as missing, and indeed the Lever Brothers magazine *"Progress"* later reported that by the 4th August his parents had still not had any definite news about him. Sadly it was eventually confirmed, and as would be expected in the circumstances, he has no known grave.

But he is commemorated on the Thiepval Memorial to the missing on the Somme.

A photo of his name on the memorial is shown here.

Percy qualified for a 1915 Star, British War Medal and Victory Medal. His parents would have received a Memorial Plaque and Scroll.

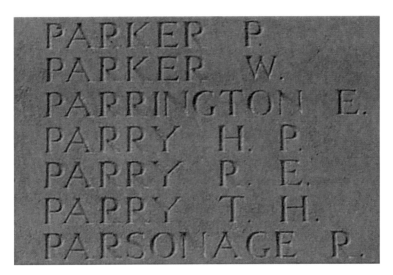

He is also commemorated on the Port Sunlight Memorial and on his parent's headstone in Christ Church, Port Sunlight.

Two of his brothers also served in the war and survived.

Arthur joined the 8th Kings Liverpool early on, and ended up as a Sergeant.

Alfred joined the Royal Field Artillery.

As a finishing touch to his story, his parents asked for permission to erect a plaque in his memory inside St.Andrews church. A photograph of it is shown here.

The plaque shows his year of birth as 1893 but birth records indicate 1894.

16251 LANCE CORPORAL HERBERT JOHN LEWIS
18th Battalion – Kings Liverpool Regiment

THE ST.ANDREWS MEMORIAL NAMES HIM as *"H. John Lewis"* so it can be assumed that he was popularly known as John.

John was born on 18th August 1892 in Port Sunlight the son of George Frederick Lewis and his wife Harriet (nee Ellis). George was originally from Herefordshire but had moved to Bebington by 1891 when he married Harriet at St.Andrew's church. Harriet was from Shropshire but she had been working as a servant in Church Road, Lower Bebington before the wedding. George was employed at Lever Brothers, first as a Labourer and later as a Tool Grinder.

The couple had five children but only 2 had survived infancy, John and his younger brother George Sydney. Sadly Harriet died in 1898 aged just 37 and the two boys who were just 4 & 5 years old were left without a mother.

IN 1901 GEORGE AND HIS TWO sons were living at 18 Park Road, Port Sunlight (see photo). George never remarried but he found a solution to his domestic problems by bringing his sister Annie to live with them as a housekeeper. The system obviously worked well because she was still there in 1911, by which time John and George were both working at Lever Brothers, John as a Shipping Clerk.

John had been a member of the Port Sunlight Boy's Brigade, and he must have started work at Levers at a young age because he had qualified as a Co-Partner before enlisting (this required 10 years service).

Enlist he did though, on 2nd September 1914 at Liverpool. He joined the 18th Battalion of the Kings Liverpool Regiment, popularly known as the 2nd Liverpool Pals. At his medical he was 5'-3½" tall and 9 stone, with hazel eyes and brown hair. He was Church of England.

During their training in the UK they came under the orders of the 30th Division and eventually embarked on board S.S. "Invicta" landing at Boulogne on 7th November 1915.

John's service record has survived and gives a lot of useful information.

In February 1916 he suffered from Scabies and had 3 days treatment by 98th Field Ambulance. He soon rejoined his unit, only to go down with Measles on 20th April, and it was 10 days this time before he was back with the Pals.

His health problems were tempered by the good news of his promotion to Lance Corporal (unpaid) in July, although he was eventually paid for this appointment in January 1917.

John got through the first day of the Somme without mishap, but lost two friends from Port Sunlight that day. Henry Hughes and Percy Parry's stories are told on the preceding pages.

On 10th August 1916 he suffered a thigh injury which was attended to by 96th Field Ambulance and it was 4th September before he was back in action again.

He attended the 30th Divisions Grenade School for a week in September 1916 and then spent another 25 days training at the Divisions Infantry School in November. To cap off this relatively enjoyable period in John's army career he received a good conduct badge on 28th November, having completed two years service. The end of 1916 was spent at the Divisional Depot, from Christmas Eve until January 5th.

John's Battalion were in the 21st Brigade of the 30th Division. In April 1917 the Germans withdrew to the Hindenberg Line and the 21st Brigade were in pursuit. On 9th April the Brigade attacked the German front line trenches south east of Arras. The following account is written using the Battalion war diary.

The Liverpool Pals were in assembly trenches south of Neuville-Vitasse and they went over the top at 11.35am, they had to advance over at least 2,000 yards of open ground. They set off in formation at first but owing to machine gun fire and considerable resistance from German positions in the sunken roads in front of them they were held up. During this time they were also under considerable artillery fire from guns of all calibres. When they had fought their way to a position in front of the German line they discovered that the barbed wire was practically uncut. Once they had got held up by the barbed wire they consolidated their position and held onto it until 3am on the 10th when they were relieved by the 16th Manchesters. All this time they had been under intense machine gun and rifle fire.

At some point during that days fierce fighting John had been killed in action at the age of 24. The war diary only listed Officers casualties for the day of 2 killed, 1 missing, and 8 wounded.

Soldiers Died in the Great War gives the figures for Other Ranks as 57 men killed in action.

John is buried in Wancourt British Cemetery, just one of nearly 2,000 Commonwealth casualties buried here – many of them unidentified.

A photograph of his headstone is shown here.

John is also commemorated on the Port Sunlight memorial, and he qualified for a 1915 Star, British War Medal, and Victory Medal.

John's father George died in 1923 aged just 56. He seems to have had little luck in his life, losing three babies, then his wife after just 7 years of marriage, and finally his eldest son to the war. It could be wondered if all the tragedies in his life had anything to do with his own early death.

On a rather happier note, John's only brother George Sydney Lewis also served in the war. He enlisted right at the start as W/411 with the 13th Cheshires (Wirral Pals). George was eventually taken a prisoner of war at Ploegsteert on 11th April 1918, and after enduring a terrible experience in the POW camp he was eventually repatriated, and eventually demobbed on 30th April 1919. He wrote a graphic account of his experiences as a POW which was published in the Levers magazine *"Progress"* in January 1919. It is an amazing story but too long to recount here.

2ND LIEUTENANT RICHARD POWELL SCHOLEFIELD
16th Battalion Cheshire Regiment

RICHARD WAS BORN ON 18th March 1885 into a wealthy family, his father Henry Ernest Scholefield was originally from South Shields, County Durham and ran his own chemical manufacturing company for many years. He had married Richard's mother Elizabeth (nee Powell) in Liverpool in 1883 and they were living there until after the turn of the century. They had moved to a grand house *"Poulton Hey"* in Spital by 1911. This was owned by one of the great Cheshire families the Lancelyn Greens and is still there today. It was eventually given to the parish of St Andrews by Roger Lancelyn Green in 1972 and is now the parish centre of Holy Trinity Church, Poulton Lancelyn. A present day photograph of the house is shown here.

The seven children of the family were : Henry, Richard Powell, Elizabeth Victoria, Stephen, Mary Isabel (died aged 5), Joyce Ray and Arthur.

The children were sent away to boarding schools and never appeared together on censuses. In 1901 Richard was 16 years old and away at King William College near Castletown on the Isle of Man.
He also attended Liverpool College, specialising in chemistry.

After completing his education Richard worked in Liverpool for his fathers chemical business Messrs. Powell & Scholefield. He played tennis and was also a member of Bromborough golf club.

Richard enlisted as 17708 Private Schofield with the 19th (City) Battalion of the Kings Liverpool Regiment in Liverpool on 3rd September 1914. His medical report revealed that he was Church of England, 5'-6½" tall, just over 8 stone in weight, with blue eyes, brown hair and a sallow complexion.

He would have started his training with what was popularly known as the 3rd Liverpool Pals Battalion soon after this.

His younger brother Stephen had also joined the 19th Kings Liverpool possibly at the same time, but what is certain is that a year later, on 4th September 1915 Richard and Stephen were both transferred to the 17th (Reserve) Battalion of the Cheshires with a view to obtaining a commission. They were allocated consecutive service numbers of 27802 & 27803. Richard's commission was official just a week later and he was appointed a 2nd Lieutenant in the 16th Battalion, Cheshires. It is believed that Stephen became a 2nd Lieutenant with the 15th Battalion.

These were both Bantams Battalions, formed specifically for men of heights 5'-0" to 5'-3" (less than the minimum 5'-3" normally required) Officers, like Richard, were more likely to be taller though!

Another photo in Officers uniform, smoking his pipe!

He did more training, most probably at Prees Heath in Shropshire before, at long last, he was posted overseas.

The 15th and 16th Bantams both arrived at Le Havre in January 1916, and Richard's service record indicates that he was free of any injuries until July.

From the 16th – 19th July 1916 the Battalion were holding trenches at Waterlot Farm, near Trones Wood. This was during the initial phase of the Somme, and the Battalions war diary gives a long and very detailed account of the often desperate fighting that took place over those few days, but an excerpt is given here covering the fatal wound received by Richard Scholefield (on the afternoon of the 18th : *"- - - artillery support had been asked for and was obtained at 4.30pm. The enemy retired leaving some snipers in shell holes who caused considerable loss until dominated by the snipers of the garrison. On the north east of the farm a company of the enemy emerged from Delville wood, and got into the German trench moving towards Guillemont. At the same time the enemy, strength one battalion, moved out of this trench in 6 lines and advanced on the farm – 2nd Lieutenant Scholefield who was at this time in command of the 2 platoons on the north east of the farm, opened fire with his Lewis gun and rapid (rifle) fire at 300 yards range – the enemy who were in very close formation did not stand this fire for long, an officer was seen trying to rally his men, but they eventually retired into the trench from which they had advanced – during this attack 2nd Lt. Scholefield was dangerously wounded, and has since died - - - "*

He had received a head wound, and would have been taken to a casualty clearing station. He didn't actually die of his injuries until 25th July (aged 31). A report of his death appeared in the *"Birkenhead News"* on 29th July and it told of a letter received by his parents from Richard's Commanding Officer : *"Lt. Scholefield's Battalion (and even more so his company) was in the thickest of the fight, and more or less held the key to the British position. This they held against long odds, the Huns twice attacking in massed formation and twice being repulsed with only the handful of men that were left. It was during the second attack that Lt. R.P. Scholefield was hit in the head and died before reaching the hospital"*

It was a torrid time for both the 15th & 16th Bantams, just a few days later on the 27th July the 15th were also in the thick of it, their war diary reporting that relentless enemy shelling had continued in the morning, and at mid-day a shell landed on an officers dugout killing 2nd Lt. Colin Dickinson and wounding 2nd Lt. Stephen Scholefield and 2nd. Lt. J.N.Watson. It seems that it could have been even worse news for the parents, but Stephen survived this injury and also the war.

IN 1917 RICHARD'S PARENTS APPLIED for permission to have a brass plaque placed in the church in his memory, and it is there to this day – see photograph.

Richard is buried in La Neuville British Cemetery, Corbie. It contains 866 Commonwealth casualties from the Great War.

The epitaph, chosen by his parents is: *"The Angel of the Lord shall lift this head"*.

Richard was awarded a British War Medal and Victory Medal.
He had never married, so his parents would also have received a Memorial Plaque and Scroll.

It should also be mentioned here that there is an excellent account of the death of Richard Scholefield (and the days action) in Stephen McGreal's book *"Cheshire Bantams"* published by Pen & Sword.

24593 PRIVATE JOSEPH JONES
10th Battalion Cheshire Regiment

JOSEPH WAS BORN IN STORETON on Christmas Day 1885, (and christened on 28th February). Joseph and his sister Jessie (4 years his senior) were born out of wedlock to Annie Jones who was of a Storeton family. Annie and her mother Ellen ran a laundry business together for many years.

They continued to live in Storeton in 1891 and 1901, but in the 1911 census Jessie was a Laundress living in Storeton on her own. Annie was 49 now and working as a servant for a Mr. Dickin in Storeton – and Joseph cannot be found on the 1911 census.

However he certainly enlisted with the 10th Cheshires at Birkenhead in 1914 or 1915. And curiously his medal card shows that he arrived in France on his 30th birthday, Christmas Day 1915! The Battalion had arrived in France on 26th September 1915 so Joseph was probably part of a reinforcement draft.

He was killed in action near Loos in France on the 21st May 1916 at the age of 30, and with no service or pension records having survived the only other information we have to go on is his medal index card and the Battalion war diary. An account of the events leading up to Joseph's death is given below.

The 10th Battalion had a spell out of the line from the 10th - 16th May, but on the morning of the 17th they took over front line trenches from the 3rd Worcesters near Mont-St-Eloi, about 5 miles north west of Arras.

At about 10pm, on the 18th May, an enemy attack was made against the Cheshire's positions. They captured some outposts and also positions being held on the lip of a shell crater. A counter-attack was organised and there was severe hand-to-hand fighting. The Cheshires managed to recapture the nearer outpost line but could not retake the crater. 1 officer and 11 other ranks were killed, and over 40 wounded.

The next day another German attack was driven back at 9.15pm, at the cost of another 10 men killed.

The 20th was a day of heavy shelling and another 14 men were killed.

And so the morning of the 21st arrived, the Cheshires communication trenches were shelled, and at 3.45pm there was another more intense bombardment that lasted for 4 hours and the entry in the war diary reads :-

"The bombardment continued with unabated violence for four hours at the end of which time most of the trenches were levelled and a very large proportion of the men killed or wounded. At 7.45pm, the enemy attacked and took our outpost and line of resistance on the left with but little resistance, this was a result of the bombardment - practically nobody was left to oppose them. A counter attack was delivered at 2am which was successful in retaking the line of resistance."

The diary gives casualty figures on this one day of, 1 officer and 33 men killed, 101 wounded and 41 missing. This was only a preliminary figure though because *"Soldiers Died in the Great War"* gives 50 officers and men killed in action, Joseph was one, most of the others were mid-Cheshire lads.

Joseph has no known grave but is remembered on the Loos Memorial. (photo shown here)

He qualified for a 1915 Star, British War Medal and Victory

Medal. And his next of kin (perhaps Jessie?) should have received a
Memorial Plaque and Scroll.

```
James Griffiths,        Name supplied by one of Storeton District. Vis-
                        will try to supply address later.
Michael Hunt,           do. Understand that Mrs.Hall
                             Storeton Hall Cottages, is
Joseph Jones, - ✓✓      do. the only relative of
                             Jos.Jones in the District.
```

The Joseph Jones written about here is a man born in Storeton, and
has no known direct link with Bebington. However, it is believed that
he is the casualty named on the memorial for the following reasons :

Next of kin data compiled for the St. Andrew's memorial in the
early 1920's confirms that Joseph Jones' name was supplied by a visitor
from Storeton, and that his only relative is Mrs. Hall of Storeton. (see
extract above).

Joseph's sister Jessie Jones married Frederick Hall in a civil marriage
in Wirral on 18th April 1914 and a tribute to Joseph printed in the
"Birkenhead News" a year after his death from the couple is shown here.

JONES—In loving memory of Pte. J. Jones, 10th Cheshires,
    killed in action May 18th, 1916.
        When last we saw him smiling
        He looked so strong and brave,
        We little thought how soon he'd be
        Laid in a hero's grave.
                        —Jessie and Fred, Storeton.

200796 PRIVATE WILLIAM BRAYNE
1/4th Battalion - Cheshire Regiment

WILLIAM HAD QUITE A SAD childhood, but things really started to improve for him until the war intervened.

He was born on 11th May 1897 in Saughall near Chester, the son of Enoch and Alice Brayne. His parents were from the Ellesmere area of Shropshire originally and Enoch was working on a farm in 1901. Alice died young in 1904, just 33 and William had lost his mother before he was 7 years old.

Enoch was obviously struggling to earn a living and also look after his 4 children, and by 1911 he was living as a boarder in Rodney Street, Birkenhead with his daughter Gladys. William and his brother Thomas *"John"* were being looked after by his auntie and uncle in their lovely house in Port Sunlight.

Their aunt Sarah was Enoch's sister and she was married to Edward Edwards, a Bricklayer at Lever Brothers.

They were living at 34 Greendale Road and the two boys were being well looked after. After Williams death his auntie referred to him as *"our dear Bill"* so he will be referred to as Bill from now on.

He had attended Port Sunlight school, and was a member of the Port Sunlight Boys Brigade. After schooling he got a job at Lever Brothers working in No.4 Woodbox Department.

On the outbreak of war he enlisted with the Cheshire Regiment at Birkenhead in November 1914, and his initial service number appears to have been 2741.

After training in the UK he was posted overseas to Egypt in early 1916. The 4th Battalion had been in Gallipoli in 1915 and Bill was lucky to have missed that experience. He did serve in Egypt and Palestine for just over 2½ years though, but in June 1918 the Battalion were posted to France.

The 4th Battalion had been at Oulchy-le-Chateau (about 10 miles south of Soissons) at least since July 25th and Bill died of wounds (aged 21) in hospital in or near Senlis which is about 35 miles to the west. So it is likely that he was wounded at least a day or so before his death and taken to hospital. It is also possible that he was gassed, because it is known that the Germans were using gas in this area.

An article in the *"Birkenhead News"* at the time of his death mentioned that he hadn't been home since he left for Egypt in 1916, but he had been expected back on leave when his aunt & uncle received the sad news of his death.

It is of interest locally that Bill died on 2nd August, and two Higher Bebington men – Robert Fairclough and James Holding (also 4th Battalion) died on 30th July and 1st August.

Bill is buried in Senlis French National Cemetery, there are just over 100 Great War casualties here and a photo of Bill's headstone is shown here.

Bill is also commemorated on the Port Sunlight memorial and on the Boys Brigade Roll of Honour in Christ Church.

He was awarded a British War Medal and Victory medal, and his next of kin (father, or aunt & uncle) would have received a Memorial Plaque and Scroll.

Bill's brother John enlisted in the 13th Cheshires at Port Sunlight on 3rd September 1915, but was discharged with a foot problem and so never served overseas.

334736 GUNNER JOHN MATTHEW HULL
350th Siege Battery – Royal Garrison Artillery

JOHN WAS BORN IN 1877 in Bebington (probably Spital). He was the son of John Hull, who was from St.Albans originally, and his wife Ann (nee Lewis).

John senior had been living and working on the farms in Spital from the 1870's at least, and he had married Ann, from Sealand, at St.Andrew's church, Bebington in 1870.

John senior and his family were living in Spital from 1871 to 1911, but he lost his wife Ann in 1900. They had seven children, Eliza, Peter, Alice, Mary Anne, John Matthew, William Robert, and Isabella Ellen.

In 1891 young John, only 13 years old, was already working as a gardener, an occupation he was still pursuing in Spital in 1901.

But by 1905 John was living in Formby and he had met Mary McAdam who had been working as a Housemaid in the town for a few years. She was from Irongray near Dumfries and on 9th June 1905 John married Mary in her home parish in Scotland.

Nothing more can be written until the 1911 census when the couple were living at North End, Halewood, Liverpool. John was still a domestic gardener and they now had two daughters. They were eventually to have four children : Mary Isabel, Agnes Annie, John and Margaret.

At the time war broke out John was working as a *"skilled gardener"* at Weston House, Halewood for a Mr. A.C. Mitchell, but he eventually enlisted with the Royal Garrison Artillery at Widnes in the autumn of 1915. He was now aged 37 or 38 and perhaps because of his age he doesn't seem to have been called up until June 1916. He then served in a home defence battery for over a year before eventually being posted to France in September 1917.

Royal Garrison Siege Batteries were equipped with heavy, large calibre guns and howitzers and were usually positioned some way behind the front line.

The 350th Battery in which John was a Gunner, was equipped with four 6" howitzers.

John's experience of life on the Western Front was to prove very short, on 27th October 1917 he was killed in action near Ypres in Belgium aged 39 or 40.

Unfortunately there is no war diary available for the 350th Siege Battery themselves at that particular time, but it is known that they were in action at the Battle of Passchendaele, and were in position north east of Ypres. However, in a war diary for the 59th H.A.G. (Heavy Artillery Group) it mentions that on 27th October :

"The personnel of 101st Siege Battery were relieved by 350th Siege Battery. This latter Battery lost 3 men killed and one wounded while taking over from 101st Siege Battery."

It is probable that they were killed by German shelling. One of the other men killed was Frederick Southern from Everton, and he is buried with John in Minty Farm cemetery, about 3 miles north of Ypres.

A photograph of John's headstone is shown here. Minty Farm Cemetery contains 192 Great War burials, more than a third of them being Royal Artillerymen.

John qualified for a British War Medal and Victory Medal. His wife Mary would also have received a Memorial Plaque and Scroll.

Shortly after the war Mary was living at Strawberry Field Lodge, Vale Road in Woolton.

There is also an army record for a 614459 Gunner William R. Hull serving in the Royal Horse Artillery. This might be John's younger brother William Robert, happily this man survived the war.

51490 PRIVATE ERNEST JAMES IVESON
5th Battalion Kings Liverpool Regiment

THE MEMORIAL BOARD NAMES HIM as E. James Iveson, and he was definitely James to his parents. They placed several tributes to him in the local newspapers after his death always referring to him as James.

He was born in Birkenhead in July/August 1898, the first of four children. The three others were Margaret, Thomas Joseph, and Esther Elizabeth.

His parents Ernest James and Margaret Iveson (nee Bowen) were from Birkenhead and had married at St. Nicholas' church, Liverpool in June 1897.

IN 1911 THE FAMILY WERE living at No.20 Gladstone Road, Lower Tranmere. The father was working at Lever Brothers though, working as a General Labourer, and he soon got a company house for his family at No.6 Greendale Road, Port Sunlight (see photo).

185

As a boy James attended Mersey Park school in Tranmere, and after the family moved to Port Sunlight he took a job in No.2 Soapery at Lever Brothers. He worked there for 4½ years until he joined the army.

James' service papers have not survived and so we cannot be certain exactly when he enlisted, but according to local newspaper reports it was probably December 1916 – January 1917.

After training in the UK he was posted overseas to the 5th Battalion Kings Liverpool Regiment in September 1917.

There are no reports of any injuries during his time in France from September 1917 until April 1918, but the *"Birkenhead News" reported that he "had practically been in action during the whole of the time until his death"*.

The Battalion war diary reported that they had been in the Festubert area since 4th April and had a pretty quiet time, with few casualties until the 9th.

A transcription of the war diary for 9th April reads :

"Just after 4am the enemy bombarded our lines with gas and high explosive shells. Morning very foggy. The enemy attacked at about 7.30pm. Two of the companies are missing and the foremost platoons of "A" company in Caillioux locality. The enemy captured the OB line but our posts at Festubert East and those in the Village Line remained intact."

No casualty figures are given in the diary, but *"Soldiers Died in the Great War"* indicates that 2 officers and 60 other ranks were killed in action on this day. Several more would no doubt have died of wounds in the next few days.

The Battalion held this line for two more days despite intense enemy bombardments, but on the 10th and 11th they only had one man killed and one died of wounds.

James, and two other men, died of wounds on 12th April and given the casualty figures quoted above it looks highly likely that he received his fatal wounds on the 9th.

He died at a nearby casualty clearing station aged just 19.

James qualified for a British War Medal and Victory Medal, and his parents would have received a Memorial Plaque and Scroll.

James is also commemorated on the Port Sunlight memorial.

He is buried in Lillers Communal Cemetery Extension and a photograph of his headstone is pictured here. The epitaph, which would have been chosen by his parents reads :

*"Sleep On Beloved
Take Thy Rest
We Loved You
But God Loved You Best"*

A lovely family photograph taken in 1916 or 1917 is shown here James with sister Margaret at the back, young Thomas on the left, and Esther between her mum and dad.

In loving memory of our dear son, Rifleman James Iveson, 1/5th K.L.R., died of wounds April 12th, 1918, and was buried at Lillers Cemetery, France.— Never forgotten by Father, Mother, Sisters and Brother, 6, Greendale-road, Port Sunlight.
    We prayed for his safe returning,
      We longed to clasp his hand,
    But God has postponed the meeting,
      It will be in the better land.

From the *"Birkenhead News"* dated 12th April 1919

12376 PRIVATE GEORGE SCHEERS
8th Battalion Cheshire Regiment

GEORGE HAS BEEN A BIT of a problem to research. On various records his surname appears as Sheirs, Shiers, Sheers, and Scheers. The author is accepting Scheers, the version used on the memorial in St. Andrews and by Lever Brothers where he worked.

George's upbringing was rather sad, and no birth record can be verified, but by using the 1901 & 1911 census and particularly his army service papers it looks most likely that he was born in Toxteth, Liverpool in March 1889.

His father James was a shoemaker from Staffordshire originally, and his mother cannot be traced mainly due to the surname problem mentioned above, but there will be more about her later.

In 1901 James and his two children Emma (13) and George (11) were living as boarders at No.14 Marquis Street, New Ferry. The head of the house was James Murphy, a self employed shoemaker. It can be safely assumed that James was working for Mr. Murphy.

James died in 1907 aged 47 and by 1911 George was working at Prices Candles in the extraction plant and he was in lodgings at 47 Manor Place, Bromborough Pool. Soon after this he took a job at Lever Brothers also in the extraction plant and he was still working there at the outbreak of war.

George volunteered for the 8th Battalion Cheshire Regiment at Birkenhead on 1st September 1914, and his service papers make interesting reading.

He was 5'-3½" tall, 8 stone 4 lbs with hazel eyes and dark brown hair. His age is given very precisely as 25 years and 157 days.

On a page listing his family members he revealed that he had no father, no grandparents, no wife, one sister Emma, and then a poignant note about his mother : *"Deserted us when babies, married again, don't know her whereabouts."*

He trained with his Battalion at Tidworth, Chisledon and Pirbright, and on 10th October he was promoted to Lance Corporal. Also while still training he spent 3 weeks in hospital in January 1915 having some varicose veins sorted out in his right leg.

In June 1915 they embarked for Egypt en route to Gallipoli. After stopping off at Alexandria they moved on to the port of Mudros on the Greek island of Lemnos by early July. The Battalion had missed out on the initial landing at Gallipoli on 25th April, but they finally arrived there, at Cape Helles, towards the middle of July. It looks as though George may have been left behind on Lemnos because he had contracted Enteritis on 15th July and was admitted to No.16 Stationary Hospital at Mudros, spending 2 weeks there before being discharged to duty.

On 20th August George was appointed an acting Corporal, and a few months later on 29th November he was admitted to No.18 Stationary Hospital with frostbite. All summer the troops had been plagued with dysentery caused by the intense heat, and George then goes down with frostbite! Anything is better than a gunshot wound though. Four weeks later he was back with his unit, who by now had been evacuated from the failed campaign at Gallipoli and were probably back at Mudros.

The Battalion remained in the area into January 1916 and it is worth recording that for one reason or another on 22nd January George relinquished his rank and reverted back to Private – at his own request.

They moved on, first to Port Said in Egypt in January and then on 14th February they embarked at Port Said for Mesopotamia (modern day Iraq), arriving at Basra on 28th February.

The British had been in the Basra area since 1914, occupying oilfields and pipelines. They were fighting the Turks, but strong resistance had cut off our army of about 9,000 men at Kut-al-Amara and they had been besieged there for 5 months. They had almost run out of supplies and disease was rife so a decision was taken to attempt a relief operation.

The Cheshires were to be involved in this attack on Turkish positions at El Hanna, about 20 miles north west of Kut-al-Amara.

The attack commenced at 4.55am on the 5th April 1916 and the plan was that the Cheshires would follow on close behind the first wave of attacking troops, but at some point they found themselves leading the attack.

The Regimental History gives a concise account of the action :

"- - - the Battalion found itself the advanced guard of the Division - - - nothing could be seen of the enemy but gradually fire was felt on the left flank and Colonel Grover changed direction toward this - - - - after moving forward some 300 yards the enemy fire became heavier, and after advancing a further 300 yards in short rushes they halted and dug in. They were quite unsupported. Here they remained until 7pm when they were relieved under cover of darkness."

The Battalion war diary reported that casualties for the day were 4 officers and 28 other ranks killed, with 7 officers and 170 other ranks wounded, and 7 men were missing.

The position was successfully assaulted an hour later by 38th & 39th Brigades, but they also *"suffered rather heavily."*

George Scheers, aged 27, was one of the Cheshire's 28 other ranks killed in action on the day, and he has no known grave. He is

commemorated on the Basra memorial though, and also on the Port
Sunlight memorial.

A photograph of the
panel on the Basra
memorial showing
George's name is
shown here.

Note the use of the
Sheers version of his
name.

George qualified for a 1915 Star, British War Medal, and Victory
Medal.

Curiously, his service record reveals that his personal possessions and
medals were sent to Miss Maggie Holden of 16 Windy Bank, Port
Sunlight (the sister of Horace Holden whose story was told earlier
in this book), but his Memorial Plaque and Scroll went to George's
married sister Emma Thompson of 34 Barry Street, Walton, Liverpool.
Perhaps Maggie was his girlfriend?

If this was true then George's bad luck continued, Maggie Holden
married a Peter Toohey in 1917, so by the time his medals were sent
out to her Maggie was married to someone else.

It is hoped that his medals are now being looked after somewhere
and that this brave but unlucky man is remembered as he deserves to
be.

SCHEERS.—Aged 27 years, Corporal George
Scheers (Extraction Plant), 17, Park Road, Port
Sunlight. Cheshire Regt.

Extract from the Lever Brothers *"Progress"* magazine – July 1916.

861 LANCE CORPORAL WALTER JOHN SEVERN
Denbigh Yeomanry

WALTER WAS BORN TOWARDS THE end of 1895 in the Willaston area. He was christened Walter John *"Severns"* and was listed with that version of his surname on the 1901 census. At that time he was living with his parents William and Lydia at Hans Hall Cottage in Neston-cum-Parkgate. His father was 71 and still working as a watchman on the railway but he appears to have died the following year. His mother Lydia was much younger, just 49 on the 1901 census although it does seem from other sources she was actually even younger than that. After 1901 any documentation (newspapers, army medal cards, headstone etc) all give the surname as Severn.

There is not much to tell about the family, but it appears that William and Lydia had five children, Caroline, Sarah, Sarah May, William, and Walter John. They were living in the Willaston/Neston/Parkgate area until 1902 when the father died, and they become *"lost"* on the 1911 census.

The next information that we can be certain about is that Walter enlisted with the Denbigh Yeomanry (later the 24th Battalion Royal Welsh Fusiliers) at Wrexham sometime in 1914 or early 1915. He was training with them up in Newcastle in 1915 and had the rank of Lance Corporal when he died unexpectedly.

His death certificate indicates that he suffered with tonsilitis for 10 days, this developed into broncho pneumonia for another 4 days, and he then died of blood poisoning 3 days later on 22nd June 1915 at the 1st Northern General Hospital in Newcastle, aged just 19 years. It also gives his civilian occupation as a Gardener and his address as Moorfields Cottages, Heath Road. Lower Bebington.

He was not at that address in 1911, but it is confirmed in a *"Birkenhead News"* report about Lydia's other son William. Commonwealth War Graves also confirms his next of kin as Mrs. Lydia Severn at 2 Moorfield Cottages, Heath Road.

 Walter did not get his photo featured in the local paper, but his death was mentioned in an article regarding his brother William's war service. His brother worked at Old Hall Farm in Hr. Bebington prior to the war and enlisted with the Cheshire Yeomanry in January 1915, fighting in Egypt and Palestine and surviving the war. His photograph was featured in the Birkenhead News and is included here for interest.

Walter is buried in St. Andrews churchyard, with an epitaph chosen by his mother of :

"Peace perfect peace"

Because Walter did not serve abroad he did not receive any medals, however his mother should have received a Memorial Plaque and Scroll.

On the kerb around the grave it mentions his mothers death on 9th September 1929 at the age of 70. It looks like she may be buried there with Walter.

MAJOR ARNOLD INMAN DRAPER
17th Kings Liverpool Regiment

ARNOLD WAS BORN IN BEBINGTON on 18th March 1881, the third child of Hugh William Draper (a leather merchant) and his wife Gertrude Isabella (nee Inman). Arnold's two brothers were Hugh Maurice and Leonard Henry. Although neither parent was from the area originally they had married at St. Andrews in 1877. Gertrude was a member of the Inman Line shipping company family (hence Arnolds middle name) and had lived at Spital Old Hall.

Gertrude tragically died at the age of 25 in 1881. The census was taken on 3rd April that year and Hugh was living as a widower with his in-laws so it looks as though Gertrude may have died giving birth to Arnold. Either way poor Arnold never knew his mother.

His father eventually re-married and was living at No. 8 Bromborough Road for over 30 years, having six more children.

Arnold had an expensive education, being sent to Rossall boarding school in Fleetwood, this may have led on to University because he cannot be found on the 1901 census. He was a keen sportsman before the war, excelling in hockey at which he played for England vs Germany in Hamburg at one point. He also played cricket for Rock Ferry and he was an enthusiastic swimmer.

By 1911 he was 30 years old and living as a boarder in Trafalgar Drive, Lower Bebington while working as a Clerk for the Bank of England in Castle Street, Liverpool. You might say the education had paid off! The first photo seems to show him in bank clerks clothing.

In 1912 he married Evelyn Mary Ward in Toxteth Park, Liverpool and they were to have two children – Joan Inman in 1913 and then John Hugh Arnold in 1916.

Arnold enlisted as 16130 Private Draper with the 17th Battalion Kings Liverpool Regiment at Liverpool on 12th September 1914. He was 33 years old and still living in Bebington. His papers inform us that he was C.of E. and 5'-9" tall, 10½ stone, with light brown hair and grey eyes.

By the 23rd November he was promoted to Lance Corporal, and then Lance Sergeant on 29th December. It looks as though he was being fast tracked to a commission and this arrived in April 1915 when he became a 2nd Lieutenant.

After this period of training he was eventually posted to France, arriving there on 4th November 1915.

He fought at the Somme in 1916, and was promoted to Captain in August 1916. He was at Arras and Messines in 1917 and buried by a shell explosion at one point, being dug out alive by his men. In

September 1917 he was promoted yet again to Major (see photo in officers uniform) before being killed at Passchendaele on 21st October 1917, aged 36.

The Battalion war diary reported that they were in the Hollebeke area a few miles south of Ypres. They were holding front line trenches from 17th – 20th October, and had a quiet time of it with just 7 men wounded in 4 days.

They were relieved at 8.30pm on the 21st by the 2nd Bedfordshires and marched west to Parrain Farm camp, arriving there at 10.30 the following morning. Arnold Draper was killed in action and 3 other men wounded on the 21st. It is not clear whether he was killed before they were relieved at 8.30pm, or if it was during the march back out of the line.

The war diary also reported that on 23rd : *"a large number of Officers and Other Ranks attended the funeral of Major A.I. Draper at Kemmel Cemetery at 2.30pm"*

His service record and probate record reveal that his wife was now living at *"Winterdyne"*, Rocky Lane, Heswall.

His personal effects were returned to his wife and they included : a wedding ring, signet ring, 2 wrist watches, a religious medallion and a pipe and tobacco pouch.

Arnold also had four half brothers (from his fathers second marriage) serving in the war. They all survived and were :

Lt. Charles N. Draper (Canadian Army Service Corps)
Squadron Commander Christopher Draper (Royal Naval Air Service) -awarded the Croix-de-Guerre with Palm after shooting down 3 German aircraft.
2nd Lt. Walter R. Draper (10th Kings Liverpool)
2nd Lt. Gerald H. Draper (4th Cheshires) – lost his right arm in France in February 1917.

Arnold is buried in Kemmel Chateau Military Cemetery, 5 miles south of Ypres, one of over 1,100 Commonwealth burials from the Great War here.

A photograph of his headstone is shown. His age is given as 35 but assuming his date of birth is correct then he was really 36.

The epitaph chosen by his wife reads :

"And thy joy no man taketh from thee. St. John"

Arnold was awarded a 1915 Star, British War Medal and Victory Medal.

His wife Evelyn should also have received a Memorial Plaque and Scroll.

THE SMITH BROTHERS - PETER JAMES AND ERNEST

THE TWO SMITH BROTHERS WERE the sons of Arthur and Alice Smith. Arthur was from Smethwick originally and changed jobs regularly. It varied from census to census as Grocer's Foreman, Insurance Agent, to Storekeeper, and at the time of the war he was a Gatekeeper at Cammell Laird Shipbuilders in Birkenhead.

In 1891 the family were living in Litherland (north Liverpool) with three children, Ernest was not yet born and Peter James was just 2 years old.

They had moved to Bootle by 1901 and by now they had a full complement of six children.

It should be pointed out that the memorial board in St. Andrews church lists Peter James as "*P. James Smith*" so it can be assumed that he was known to family and friends as James, so that is what he will be called on these pages.

James was born on 30th January 1889 and Ernest on 3rd January 1894, both boys were educated at Salisbury Road County Council School in Bootle.

James was a good singer and was in the choir at St. Matthew's church in Bootle for several years, singing solo on occasions.

The 1911 census revealed that the family were now living at 62 Oakleigh Grove, Lower Bebington (see photo), at which point the father was working as an Engineers Storekeeper. The parents had had ten children but six were still surviving and they were, in birth order : Arthur, Edwin, Mary, Peter James, Ernest and Elsie.

There were only two children still at home now though, and 17 year old Ernest was working as a Clerk at Lever Brothers. His older brother James was now probably far away in Chile!

After his schooling James worked in the Corn Exchange in Liverpool for Norman Thomas Bros. and he did very well with them, eventually travelling to Chile where he was employed as a Corn Merchant for Messrs. Williamson, Balfour & Co. for several years.

He then took up *"A position of trust"* with Don Thomas A. Mackay of Chile. James travelled home in the spring of 1916 to enlist with the 4th Dragoon Guards.

Ernest left Lever Brothers sometime after 1911 and started work for Cammell Laird Shipbuilders, in the Joiners shop, and he enlisted in the army in August 1915.

The story of the brothers' army service continues on the following pages.

104936 GUNNER ERNEST SMITH
"B" Battery : 70th Brigade : Royal Field Artillery

ERNEST WAS WORKING AT Cammell Laird when he joined up in August 1915.

He enlisted with the Royal Field Artillery, and after a relatively short period of training in the UK he was posted to France on 27th December 1915. This date is significant because it meant that he would eventually qualify for a 1915 Star with just four days to spare!

There are no service papers available for Ernest and so there is little information on him until the time of his death – 19th April 1917. The 70th Brigade were a part of the 15th (Scottish) Division and were at the Somme in 1916, fighting at Pozieres, Fleurs-Courcelette and Le Transloy. It is likely that Ernest was with them throughout these battles.

The following year on 9th April 1917 the Battle of Arras started, and 15th Division were involved from the off.

The 70th Brigade war diary reveals that they were at Feuchy, and from 16th – 18th April they had a pretty quiet time of it, merely reporting that Feuchy was shelled lightly on the first two evenings.

On the 19th the diary simply reports : *"Preparing for fresh attack. 71st Brigade R.F.A. join 70th Brigade R.F.A. and form left sub-group. Forward communications prepared."*

The following day all Batteries were heavily shelled.

Ernest was probably killed by German shelling on the 19th April and he is buried in Feuchy Chapel British Cemetery, Wancourt, about 4 miles east of Arras. He was 23 years old, a photograph of his headstone is shown here.

Ernest qualified for a 1915 Star, British War Medal, and Victory medal.

His parents would have received a Memorial Plaque and Scroll.

Just 16 months later they were to lose another son James.

100938 PRIVATE PETER JAMES SMITH
2nd Squadron - Machine Gun Corps - Cavalry

AS MENTIONED IN THE FAMILY details, James was working in Chile when war was declared. His service papers did not survive the London Blitz of 1940, but other documents reveal that he enlisted with the 4th Dragoon Guards in May of 1916.

He would have trained with them in the UK, but it is believed that he did not get posted overseas until as late as December 1917.

At the time he arrived in France, or possibly later, he was transferred to the Machine Gun Corps (Cavalry) and he was in the 2nd Squadron.

They in turn were attached to the 2nd Cavalry Brigade of the 1st Cavalry Division.

There were three cavalry regiments in 2nd Brigade, the 4th Dragoon Guards, 9th Lancers, and 18th Hussars – but unfortunately it is not known which one James' machine-gun squadron was attached to.

The action they were about to take part in on the 21st and 22nd August 1918 was the Battle of Albert, which was the start of what would become known as the 2nd Battle of the Somme.

The plan of action was for the 2nd Cavalry Brigade to closely follow the 3rd Australian Infantry Division, who were advancing to the line of the railway from Courcelles-le-Comte to Achiet-le-Grand, and once the infantry had reached their objective they were to take advantages of any opportunities that might present themselves. Hopefully to push through and hold more advanced positions until the infantry could come up and take over. It didn't work out to plan however.

Using the war diaries of the 2nd Squadron Machine Gun Corps and the 4th Dragoon Guards the following is an account of what actually happened on that day.

Early on the very foggy morning of 21st August the Brigade were in a position about 1 mile NNW of Fonquevillers. At 4.30 am they moved off to a concentration area in Jewel valley, south west of Ayette, arriving there at 6.10am. The 18th Hussars moved forward immediately and 4th Dragoon Guards followed at about 8.40am.

By 9.10am the position had become unclear and the Dragoon Guards were ordered to withdraw whilst three patrols were sent out to ascertain the situation. By 11am the patrols returned, reporting that the 3rd Infantry had not yet reached the line of the railway. The Machine Gun Corps withdrew at 5.30pm and the whole of the Brigade were withdrawn by about 7.30pm and moved back via Souastre to billets in Sarton, all having arrived there by 2am on the 22nd. The Machine Gun Corps diary reported the casualties for 2nd Squadron (all from shell fire) as :

4 Other Ranks killed, 2 O/R died of wounds, 28 O/R wounded, 3 O/R missing believed killed, and 77 Horses killed or wounded.

At some point during the day James was killed by shell fire aged 29.

The *"Birkenhead News"* published part of a letter of sympathy sent to James' parents which throws more light on his death. His Commanding Officer Lt. S.G. Hibbert wrote :

"The squadron was in action on that day (21st August) and while we were dismounted in a valley, after advancing a certain distance, a shell dropped in amongst the section, killing your son and one other, wounding several others and killing 14 horses. He suffered no pain, as he was killed instantaneously." The officer went on to say that with James' death he had lost one of the very best.

Arthur and Alice had already lost Ernest 16 months previously, and now another of their four sons had been killed.

James is buried close to where he fell, in Achiet-le-Grand Communal Cemetery Extension. There are over 1,200 Commonwealth casualties buried here, and a photo of James' headstone is shown here.

He qualified for a British War Medal and Victory Medal, and his parents would have received a Memorial Plaque and Scroll.

M2/073114 PRIVATE JOHN NORMAN AUSTIN
Royal Army Service Corps

RELYING ON THE MEMORIAL TABLET inscription, it would appear that he was popularly known as Norman.

He was born in 1884 in Ruabon the son of John and Gwen Austin and was one of five children, Catherine Hannah, Edward Lewis, Winifred Maude, John Norman and George Victor. The family were still living in North Wales in 1891, then they seem to have disappeared off the census records for 1901 but they were living at No.1 Windy Bank, Port Sunlight on the 1911 census.

On 1ˢᵗ May 1906 Norman married Constance Houghland in West Derby Register Office. The marriage certificate tells us that he was an Engine Cleaner living at 10 Albany Road, Stoneycroft, Liverpool and Constance was at 21 Highfield Road, Stoneycroft. A son Norman Ernest followed later that year.

Norman joined the 4th West Lancashire Howitzer Brigade of the Royal Field Artillery on 1st June 1908, and completed 3 years service, reaching the rank of Corporal at one point. On the termination of his engagement in 1911 his address was given as No.1 Windy Bank, Port Sunlight (living with his parents).

When war was declared Norman quickly enlisted with the 8th Lancashire Battery of the Royal Field Artillery on 11th September 1914, and his service record gives his address at that time as No.8 Briarwood Road, Aigburth Vale and he was working as a motor driver (chauffeur) for a Mrs Graham.

He was transferred from the RFA to the Army Service Corps on 30th March 1915 and trained with them for nearly 6 months before embarking at Avonmouth (Bristol) on 17.9.15 and arriving at Rouen (via Le Havre) three days later where he was posted to the Base Motor Transport Depot.

His next destination was Salonika, leaving Marseilles on 21st January 1916 and serving there until 25th June.

It may perhaps be imprudent to mention this, but Norman's service record lists a series of misdemeanours – from smoking on parade to at least 5 cases of being absent without leave. I think army life was getting a bit strict for him! Most of these were during 1917 and he seems to have been based in the UK for much of that year.

On 11th January 1918 he embarked at Southampton destined for Italy, and he spent the rest of the war there. Norman was still there in January 1919 when he was taken seriously ill. He was taken to 39th Casualty Clearing Station on 28th and died 2 days later at Vicenza on 30th January 1918, aged 34 or 35.

His service record states bronchial pneumonia as the cause, after having had a bout of flu. It would almost certainly have been what was later called the Spanish Flu which killed millions of people worldwide during 1918 & 1919.

Norman is buried in Montecchio Precalcino Communal Cemetery Extension, just one of 439 Commonwealth servicemen here.

He was awarded a 1915 Star, British War Medal and the Victory Medal. His wife Constance would have also received a Memorial Plaque and Scroll.

1085 SAPPER PHILIP SHONE
1st Cheshire Field Company - Royal Engineers

PHILIP WAS BORN IN THE summer of 1897 (probably July) in Macefen near Malpas. He was one of five children born to Ambrose George Shone and his wife Sarah (nee Venables). Ambrose was earning his living as a Gardener, and the family were always based around the Malpas area of south Cheshire. The children in birth order were : Ambrose George (jr.), Walter, Philip, Albert, and Thomas.

They were living in Macefen in 1901 with their first three children and Philip was 3 years old. His age tallies with the birth records for 1897, but by the time of the next census Philip had left home and was living and working as a Cowman at a farm owned by Elizabeth Clutton in nearby Tushingham. The snag is, the census declared his age as 16 when he was really only 13! More of this later though.

Meanwhile his parents were still living in Macefen with children Ambrose George, Albert and Thomas.

So Philip had made the break from home at a very young age, and at this point it was not possible to connect him to Bebington. Archive papers from the period listing next of kin details for the men on the memorial had a note *"Will try and obtain"* but fortunately at this point the research took an upward turn!

Most army service records from the Great War were stored in London, and nearly three quarters of them were destroyed by fire in the 1940 London Blitz.

210

But luckily Philip's had survived, and sure enough he listed his address as No.3 The Grove, Lower Bebington. On the 1911 census this address was occupied by the Cattrall family so Philip may have been boarding with them?

Going back again to his age, on his enlistment papers of 7th June 1915 he declared his age as 21 years 11 months. He was actually only 17 years 11 months. Perhaps Philip was unsure of his real age? However, the War Graves Commission do give his age as 19 when he was killed in November 1916, and this agrees with his birth details.

It seems that Philip had been working locally as a Platelayer on the railways (otherwise known as a Trackman - maintaining rails, sleepers, etc) and he enlisted with the Cheshire Field Company of the Royal Engineers at Birkenhead as mentioned previously. His experience of working on the railways would have been useful to the Royal Engineers.

In the absence of a photo his army medical reveals that he was 5'-7½" tall.

After training in the UK he soon embarked on the S.S. *"Lydia"* at Southampton on 2nd November 1915. He finally arrived with his unit in France on 6th November.

His service record reveals just one misdemeanour, on 23rd February 1916 he was late on parade and was given 1 day Field Punishment No.2. This usually consisted of being tied to a fixed object, such as a gun wheel for a few hours.

Philip was killed in action on the Somme on 4th November 1916, but because he had no relations on the Wirral there was no-one to send his photograph to the local press, and of course there was no other news of him either.

However the Company's war diary tells a little bit more about his final days.

They were at Courcelles-au-Bois in France, and it appears from reading the war diary to have been a quiet time. From the 1st – 4th November they were engaged in cleaning & draining trenches, water supply duties, road repairs, and erecting a drying shed in Courcelles. There was no mention of any casualties until the end of the month when the diary almost casually referred to 4th November :

"1 Officer wounded, 6 Other Ranks killed and 8 wounded (2 since died)"

Of the other 5 men of the Cheshire Field Company killed that day, three of them were from the Wirral, including George Devaney from Greasby whose death was announced in the *"Birkenhead News"* on 9th December alongside Philip's. All six of them are buried side by side in Courcelles-au-Bois Communal Cemetery Extension about 8 miles north of Albert.

This is a small cemetery containing just 115 Commonwealth casualties from the Great War, and a photograph of Philip's headstone is shown here. The epitaph chosen by his parents was :

"And in God's Roll of Honour
I hope my boy is found
Holy Jesus
Thy will be done"

Philip qualified for a 1915 Star, British War Medal, and Victory Medal and his parents would have recived a Memorial Plaque and Scroll.

Roll of Honour.

KILLED.

Cheshire Regt.—Captain R F Wolsten-holme.

Royal Engineers.—Sapper G Devaney 1376 (Greasby, Birkenhead); Sapper P Shone 1085 (Bebington).

K/24163 STOKER 1ST CLASS JOSEPH HENRY SMEDLEY
Royal Navy

JOSEPH IS NAMED AS *"HENRY"* on the memorial tablet, but in the many tributes to him in the local papers after his death he was always referred to as Harry by his family & friends, so that is what he will be called here.

He was born on 13th November 1894 in Tranmere, the oldest child of Alfred Smedley (a Baker) and his wife Mary Caroline – both born in Birkenhead.

They moved to The Rake, in Bromborough about 1899, and again to No.20 The Village, Lower Bebington by 1911.

The children of the marriage were : *"Harry"*, Doris, Ethel, Alfred Ernest and Charles Stanley. He soon decided on a naval career because on the 1911 census 16 year old Harry was already a Ships Fireman.

Some time after this, but before the start of the war, the whole family moved to Canada. The father Alfred was working at the Canmore Bakery in Alberta but in November 1914 Harry (just turning 20 now) returned home to the UK to join the Royal Navy as a Stoker. The photograph shows him with a *"H.M.S.Victory"* cap. This was actually the training barracks in Portsmouth, not the famous ship's name, and Harry is probably 20 years old in the photo.

Little more is known about him until the first quarter of 1916 when he married Martha Cliffe of Legh Road, New Ferry at St.Mark's church.

Harry served on the armoured cruiser *"H.M.S. Hampshire"* and therein lies a remarkable story.

The Hampshire fought at the Battle of Jutland on 31st May 1916 and Harry was on board. As soon as the battle was over she was ordered to take Lord Kitchener on an important diplomatic mission to Russia. At 4.40pm on Monday 5th June she left Scapa Flow (Orkney Islands) heading west into very stormy weather and joined up with her two escort destroyers *"H.M.S.Victor" and "H.M.S. Unity."* Unfortunately the two destroyers were having great difficulty keeping up with the Hampshire in what was a force 9 gale and by 6.30pm both destroyers were ordered to return to base for shelter.

The Hampshire was also struggling to make headway, and at 7.40pm her position was between Marwick Head and the Brough of Birsay. Suddenly an explosion on the port side shook the whole ship and she immediately began to sink, the steering was completely out of action and all power had gone so she was unable to make calls for assistance. Just 10 or 15 minutes after the explosion she went down, bow first.

Apparently all offers of assistance from the R.N.L.I. were turned down by the Navy, and any civilians who offered to help were told in no uncertain terms to go back to their homes.

JUST THREE CARLEY RAFTS WERE able to be launched from the Hampshire and one of them reached shore at 1am. Apparently it originally had 40 men on board and had picked up another 30 in the water, but by the time it made dry land only 6 were still alive due to exposure. It was a similar story with the other two rafts, and altogether there were only 12 survivors from the ship's complement of 655, plus 7 others who were Lord Kitchener and his staff.

Apparently on 23rd May a German submarine, the U75, had laid 22 mines around the west coast of the Orkneys and it looks likely that it was one of these that sank the Hampshire. There were a few conspiracy theories about this disaster, with talk of a German spy being on board and another suggesting that the Government wanted rid of Kitchener. The U75 seems to be the most likely culprit though.

Harry, being a Stoker, may well have been in the engine room in which case he would almost certainly have been trapped on board. He was just 21.

Just over 100 bodies were recovered and most are buried in a communal grave in Lyness cemetery, Orkney.

All the casualties are commemorated on the Portsmouth Naval memorial and a photo is shown of the panel with Harry's name on it.

Harry qualified for a 1915 Star, British War Medal and Victory Medal.

Very sadly, his young widow Martha also died on 31st October 1918 from pneumonia, aged just 23.

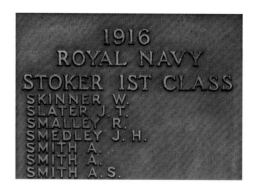

31043 PRIVATE JOHN NICHOLAS WARD
8th Battalion South Lancashire Regiment

JOHN WAS BORN IN RUNCORN in February 1898, one of nine children born to John & Eva Annie Ward. The parents were from Runcorn originally, the father being a Monumental Mason in 1901.

They moved to Bebington in about 1902, probably at the time John senior took the post of Sexton in Bebington cemetery. On the 1911 census they were living at the beautiful Sexton's Lodge on the Townfield Lane entrance of the cemetery with their eight surviving children Ethel Margaret, John Nicholas, Marion Elizabeth, Eva Doris, James Edward, Thomas Herbert, Florence Margaret and Lilian Nina.

After his death his family remembered him in the local newspapers as *"Our Jack"* so from now on he will be referred to here as Jack.

Having completed his schooling he joined Lever Brothers in Port Sunlight in August 1915, working in the Stamping Department of No.2 Soapery. He was nearing his enlistment age though, and he did this with the 14th Battalion Cheshires as 36861 Private John Ward at Birkenhead on 26th February 1916.

His service record gives his height as 5'-3¼" but not much else other than that he was mobilised on 25th April. After his training he was posted overseas to France on 30th August 1916.

He wasn't to get much experience with the 9th Cheshires though because he was transferred to the 8th Battalion South Lancashire Regiment a few weeks later on September 7th. It is likely that they were in more desperate need of reinforcements than the Cheshires were.

A good photo of Jack could not be found, and another poor one is shown here. A poor picture is better than no picture at all though?

Jack spent the winter of 1916/17with the South Lancashires, and his service record does not report any injuries or mishaps during this time.

However the 8th South Lancs were to take part in the Battle of Messines in June 1917. They were at Wulverghem in Belgium (about 6 miles south of Ypres) on 6th and at 9.30pm the Battalion moved into assembly trenches.

The following morning they took part in an attack on German positions between Messines and Wytschaete. They were in action for two days but the war diary just gives an account of casualties, which were : 1 officer killed & 6 wounded plus 25 other ranks killed, 118 wounded, and 16 missing.

Jack was one of the men killed on the 7th June 1917 aged just 19. The local newspapers reported that a German shell landed no more than a yard or so from him and his death was instantaneous. The Lever Brothers company magazine reported the same detail and described him as a well liked, promising young man who would be sadly missed in Port Sunlight and Bebington.

WALTON F. P.
WANDS J. C.
WARBURTON C.
WARD J. N.
WATERS J.
WATERWORTH J.
WATSON J.

If the report that a shell landed a yard away from him is correct then it would easily, but gruesomely, explain why he has no known grave.

He is commemorated on the Menin Gate in Ypres, which lists the names of nearly 55,000 soldiers whose bodies were never found.

A photograph of the panel with his name on is shown here.

Jack is also commemorated on the Port Sunlight memorial. He qualified for a British War Medal and Victory Medal, and his parents received a Memorial Plaque and Scroll.

23268 CORPORAL HENRY DAVIES MM
1st Battalion - Cheshire Regiment

THE MEMORIAL TABLET IN ST. ANDREWS lists him as *"Henry Davies MM"* (the MM signifying that he had won the Military Medal). However he appears to have been christened Harry and was always known as Harry to his family and friends.

He was born in Willaston in 1898 to William Davies, a Farm Worker, and his wife Mary. The couple had at least 10 children : Edward, Eleanor, Thomas William, Emily, Elizabeth Jane, William, Harry, George, Louise, and Samuel.

On the 1901 census the large family were living in Raby, but by 1911 they were at Claremont Cottages, Spital. By now the two eldest children had left home and Emily and Elizabeth were working at Lever Brothers. Harry was 12 and still at school.

However, sometime after leaving school he started work in the Timber Stores at Levers, working there until he joined the army. At this point the research becomes difficult to say the least, there are no service papers surviving and nothing appeared for him in the local papers - except for a note about the award of his Military Medal.

He joined the Cheshire Regiment and his medal index card indicates that he did not get posted overseas before January 1916, but this is not surprising given his age. Officially, men under the age of 19 should not have been sent out of the UK, although this rule was sometimes overlooked. The best estimate is that Harry may have enlisted in 1916 and after his training been posted to France in 1917.

There was one small article about his death in the Lever Brothers company magazine *"Progress"* that mentioned him being wounded on October 3rd 1917 (at Passchendaele) and then wounded again in May 1918. The article reported him as being in the 3rd Battalion but this was just his Training Battalion, he was actually serving in France and Belgium with the 1st Battalion.

His injury in May 1918 could possibly have been when he won his Military Medal. The citation as to how and when he won it could not be found, but the award was announced in the *"London Gazette"* on 12th June and then in the *"Birkenhead News"* on 19th.

MILITARY MEDALLISTS.

The following local awards of Military Medals have been made :—

Bryan, 15755, Sergt. E. E., Liverpool Regiment (Prenton).

Davies, 23268, Pte., Cheshire Regiment (Spital).

Typically, the notice in the *"London Gazette"* would appear 2 or 3 months after the act of bravery was performed.

This award would probably have been followed by his promotion to Corporal.

The 1st Cheshires were a part of 5th Division, and they were all transferred to Italy at the end of January 1918 in order to help our Italian allies who were fighting the Austro-Hungarians. The Cheshires were based alongside the River Piave which runs from the Alps down

to the Adriatic near Venice. The soldiers were reported to be happy with their new posting, and after enduring the horrors of Passchendaele just a few months before who can blame them. During about 2 months in Italy they had only lost 5 men in action.

It wasn't to last however and as soon as the German Spring Offensive started on 21st March 1918 they were hurriedly recalled to the Western Front.

HARRY WAS KILLED IN ACTION on the 23rd October 1918 during the Allies final advance in Picardy, it was known as the Battle of the Selle and the 1st Cheshires were heavily involved in an attack on the village of Beaurain on that day.

Beaurain is about 15 miles east of Cambrai.

The Battalion suffered heavy casualties from German shelling while getting to their assembly positions at around midnight on the 22nd, but by 1.30am they were finally in position.

At 3.20am on the 23rd the Cheshires were ordered to advance. The enemy immediately opened fire with machine guns and artillery, and while the Cheshires were crossing no mans land a few Germans left their own trench and met them with fixed bayonets. These were dealt with by the Cheshire's leading waves. The German machine guns were positioned in a sunken road but were eventually overpowered. The Cheshires pressed on and had taken their final objective before 9am when the 1st Norfolks came through and advanced 100 yards beyond them. At 10.05 am the 13th Rifle Brigade also passed them, meeting little resistance.

The Cheshires had captured 5 machine guns and taken 47 prisoners, and having done their job well they were ordered to withdraw to Caudray at 3.30pm.

According to the Battalion war diary the Cheshires had lost 1 officer & 34 men in the attack, with another 177 wounded. *"Soldiers Died in the Great War"* gives 43 men killed in action.

Corporal Harry Davies was one of those killed, aged just 20.

He is buried in Amerval Communal Cemetery Extension, Solesmes, and 28 of his comrades who fell that day are buried here with him, several of them alongside him. There are a total of 150 Commonwealth casualties here.

A photograph of his headstone is shown here.

Apart from his Military Medal Harry also qualified for a British War Medal and a Victory Medal. His parents would have received a Memorial Plaque and Scroll.

Harry is also commemorated on the Port Sunlight Memorial.

MAJOR WILLIAM ERNEST WATSON D.S.O.
6th Dragoon Guards

HE IS NAMED ON THE memorial tablet in St. Andrew's church as *"W. Ernest Watson"* and so he will be referred to here as Ernest.

Ernest was born on 5th September 1876 in Rock Ferry, the son of William Watson (a Cotton Broker) and his wife Jane Stock Watson. His father had been born in Charleston U.S.A. and his mother was from Liverpool.

In 1881 the family were living at No.2 Rock Park in Rock Ferry employing three servants. There were five children : Eliza Torrenza, Catherine Yaddie, Harriet, William Ernest and Stephen Leonard. By 1891 they had moved to *"Lancelyn"* in Spital Road, Bebington. Three children were at home, including Ernest aged 13, they were now employing six servants.

Ernest was a career soldier and appears to have joined the 6th Dragoon Guards (the *"Carabiniers"*) as a 2nd Lieutenant in 1897. He was progressively promoted to Lieutenant in 1899, Captain in 1901, and finally to Major on 23rd April 1910.

He served in the 2nd Boer War from 1899 – 1902 and was awarded a Queens Medal with 6 clasps and a Kings Medal with 2 clasps, and was also Mentioned in Dispatches. He was awarded the Distinguished Service Order in 1901 for rendering *"Special and Meritorious Service"* in the war.

From South Africa the Regiment moved straight to India in 1903 and remained there until 1908. During this period, on 14th September 1905 Ernest married Florence Daisy Sillitoe Treanor at Holy Trinity church in Bangalore.

The Dragoon Guards were later back in South Africa, where their first child Monica Constance was born in 1909 in the Orange Free State.

The Regiment finally returned to the UK in 1912 and were based in Canterbury, where their second and final child, Margaret Nancy was born in 1913.

With the Regiment now conveniently based in the UK they were posted to France almost as soon as war was declared, arriving there on 19th August 1914.

Ernest was only at the front for just over two months before he was killed in action on 31st October 1914 at the age of 38.

The 6th Dragoon Guards were in Belgium and had spent a few days in billets at Wytschaete. At 4am on the morning of 26th they marched out and took over trenches west of Oosttaverne from Indian Infantry, having a pretty quiet time of it. The next three days they remained in these trenches and were heavily shelled on 28th. This heavy shelling continued the following day from 9am to dusk, at which time they were ordered to withdraw to a new line between Wytschaete and Messines. On 30th they were shelled all day from 10am with shrapnel and high explosives but thankfully they had a quiet night.

And so the morning of 31st dawned, a transcript of the Regimental war diary follows :

"Enemy started shelling early in the morning and very heavy shelling continued all day. During the morning our line was reinforced by part of London Scottish, who remained in support in our rear. At dusk a

German band could be heard in the distance playing their national anthem. Nothing happened up to midnight"

But something certainly had happened, Ernest Watson was killed in action along with 19 other ranks. The war diary is understated to say the least and it seems very odd that the death of a Major passed unnoticed in the war diary.

Ernest has no known grave, but he is commemorated on the Menin Gate at Ypres. A photograph from the panel with his name on it is shown here.

The Menin Gate carries the names of more than 54,000 Commonwealth casualties of the Great War, who were killed in the fighting around Ypres but have no known grave.

Ernest qualified for a 1914 Star (with clasp), British War Medal, and Victory Medal. His widow Florence would have received a Memorial Plaque and Scroll.

After the war the planning of the memorial started. At a meeting of the committee held on 11th August 1921 a letter was read out from Mrs.Watson (presumably his mother, who was still living in the Spital/ Dibbinsdale area). She was concerned as to whether Ernest's name would be on the memorial, because he hadn't lived in the area for over 20 years. The secretary replied that it would be because he *"had been so closely connected with the Parish all of his life."*

PRIVATE 6952 JOHN LEA STATHAM
11th Battalion Australian Infantry

THE LEVER BROTHERS MAGAZINE *"PROGRESS"* referred to him as Jack Statham and so that is also what he will be called here. He was born in January 1889 in the Stockport area.

His parents Alfred Ernest Statham and Hannah Jane (nee Lea) were both born in the Manchester area and their five children were also all born there, living in Stockport in 1891. The children, in birth order were Ernest, Frederick, Ethel Lea, John Lea, and Samuel.

By 1901 they had arrived in Port Sunlight and the

father was working as a Clerk in the Costs department at Lever Brothers. They were living in a Company house, No.35 Pool Bank, and a recent photo of the house is shown here. It is also worth mentioning that Alfred had qualified as a Co-Partner at the company by the time of Jack's death.

Young Jack was only 12 years old on the 1901 census, but perhaps he was showing signs of developing an adventurous nature?
It is likely that he started work at Lever Brothers soon after this because his older brother Frederick and sister Ethel were already working there, both as Clerks.

Jack was still only 20 when he married Bertha Peirce at Salford in the last quarter of 1909. Perhaps she was his childhood sweetheart from his days living in Stockport, but what is certain is that they very soon immigrated to Australia because they are both missing from the 1911 census.

Jack and Bertha had settled into their new life in Australia by the time war was declared. Jack was employed as a Railway Guard and they may well have been living in Coode Street, Bayswater, Western Australia, because that is their address in 1916 when Jack joined up. They had three sons in Australia, John Stephen ("Jackie") in 1912, Alfred in 1914, and Frederick in 1916.

There is a bit of confusion on his service papers as to when he actually joined the army. He attested at Merriden, Western Australia on 14th March 1916, but his service history only starts on 20th June. Presumably that is when he was actually mobilised.

His medical reveals that he was 5'-7½" tall and weighed 12 stone. He was of dark complexion with blue eyes, dark hair and had a tattoo on his right forearm. His religion was Church of England.

After a period of training in Australia he embarked on the Australian transport ship "Berrima" at Fremantle on Boxing Day. The following day they were at sea and he was appointed an acting Sergeant for the duration of the voyage.

Towards the end of the long journey he suffered with a bout of Influenza before arriving at Devonport on 16th February 1917. A few days later they were with the 3rd Australian Training Battalion.

On 22nd May they arrived at Southampton, via Durrington, and boarded a transport ship to Le Havre, arriving there the next day. Jack was part of a reinforcement draft, and finally arrived with his unit on 15th June.

He appears to have had a relatively uneventful time until 1st October 1917.

The Australians were now at the Battle of Passchendaele (3rd Battle of Ypres) and moved to Westhoek Ridge on the 1st to relieve the 47th Battalion. The war diary recorded that the relief was carried out without casualties, but by the end of the day it was also reported that 2 other ranks were wounded and 3 men gassed.

Jack could have qualified on either count because he had been gassed and also suffered gunshot wounds to his ankle. He was treated by the 3rd Australian Field Ambulance and transferred to the 3rd Australian Casualty Clearing Station before being admitted to the 2nd Australian General Hospital at Wimereux on 3rd October where he was reported as dangerously ill. He died later the same day, aged 28, presumably from the effects of gas.

Jack was buried in Wimereux Communal Cemetery. There are over 2,800 Commonwealth casualties of the Great War here, most of them died of wounds in the many hospitals nearby on the coast. It is unusual in that all the headstones are laid flat on top of the graves due to the sandy nature of the soil here, a photo is shown below.

Jack qualified for a British War Medal and a Victory Medal, and

Bertha received a Memorial Plaque and Scroll. She remarried in 1919 and so his medals and plaque were addressed to Mrs. Bertha Tillett, 26 Forrest Street, Boulder City, Western Australia.

Jack is also commemorated on the Port Sunlight memorial. It can only be assumed that, as speculated previously, he did work there before emigrating.

Jack's wife Bertha originally requested the following lengthy epitaph on his headstone :

"In dreams we see our dear Daddy's face and kiss his gentle brow, but in our hearts we know we have no Daddy now. Inserted by his loving wife Bertha, and children Jackie, Alfred and Freddie"

In a letter dated March 1922 the Australian army explained to her that it was far too long and only 66 letters (including spaces) could be fitted in.

Unfortunately perhaps, Bertha never did shorten it (see photo).

Jack had two brothers who also served in the war (and survived).

Fred (pictured) had worked at Lever Brothers and had been a keen rugby player before the war. He was a Sergeant in the Royal Engineers, Fred was posted to France on 11th December 1914 and seemed to have got through the war without so much as a scratch before being de-mobbed in February 1919.

It is not known what regiment his other brother Sam served in, but he was in Africa for most of the war.

345279 PRIVATE JAMES STANLEY PEARSON
24th Battalion - Royal Welsh Fusiliers

HE IS NAMED AS *"J. Stanley Pearson"* on the memorial tablet in St. Andrews church, so it would seem that he was known to one and all as Stanley.

He was born in the first quarter of 1890, probably February, and was the only son of James Pearson, a Book Keeper, and his wife Georgina. The father appears to have been born in Wilmslow but he was married and living in Higher Bebington on the 1891 census. Stanley was just a year old.

Sadly James died sometime between 1897 and 1900 (still in his thirties), and by 1901 his widow Georgina was living at No.1 Ashbrook Terrace in Lower Bebington with all six of her children, plus two boarders. Stanley's older sister Ethel, now 17 was employed as a Bookbinder. The children in birth order were Ethel, Janet Paterson, Lilian, James Stanley, Florence and Edith.

By now Stanley was working at Lever Brothers as a Labourer, and on 27th August 1910 he married Ethel Edwards Smith in a Register Office. On the following years census they were living with Stanley's older sister Ethel at No.12 Birch Road in Lower Bebington. Ethel had married Arthur Bradley at Christ Church in Port Sunlight in 1908. Stanley's younger sisters were also living there, and conveniently his

mother Georgina was living next door at No.10 with her other two eldest daughters (both now working at Lever Brothers). STANLEY AND ETHEL HAD TWO children before he went off to the war, Leslie in 1912 and Mabel Janet in 1914. They were living at No.41 Boundary Road in Port Sunlight now (see photo), and Stanley was employed as a Fireman at Levers.

Stanley volunteered almost straight away, on 1st September 1914 as 12446 Private Pearson in the 8th Battalion Cheshire Regiment. However he was discharged as medically unfit just a month later. This was not uncommon in the early months of the war, the army could still afford to be very picky, but things changed when the casualties started mounting up. And sure enough on 5th May 1915 Stanley again attested, at Wrexham this time, as No. 1158 with the Denbighshire Yeomanry. His medical revealed that he was 5'-8" tall and 10st 4lbs, with sallow complexion, hazel eyes and black hair. He was also C.of E.

He trained in the UK at first in what was a mounted division, but in November 1915 they became a dismounted unit before finally being posted overseas on 3rd March 1916.

They embarked on board the Transport ship *Haverford* (pictured) at Devonport and their destination was Egypt.

They disembarked at Alexandria on 15th March and were to be in North Africa (and maybe Palestine) until April 1918. An important change for the Denbigh Yeomanry came in about February 1917 when they effectively became the 24th Battalion of the Royal Welsh Fusiliers, and Stanley's army number became 345279.

They left the heat of Alexandria on 29th April and disembarked in France on 7th May 1918. The Battalion were soon transferred to 94th Brigade in 31st Division on 21st June.

There is little else to report about Stanley until his death from wounds on 12th September 1918 at the age of 28. The following account is based on the Battalion war diary.

By 11pm on 4th September they had moved to a position east of Bailleul, reporting that the transport lines were being heavily shelled during the night. The following day they relieved 1st Leinsters at Hill 63 near Ploegsteert and two of their companies were in front line trenches with the other two in support. The diary reported intermittent shelling throughout the 24 hours and they had suffered 1 man killed and 4 men wounded.

Stanley's service record reveals that on this day he suffered a shell wound (this would be shrapnel) causing a compound fracture to his left thigh, so he was one of the 4 men wounded by the shelling.

He was treated at 62nd Casualty Clearing Station at Arneke in France. His wife Ethel (still at Boundary Road) received a telegram several days later warning that he was *"dangerously ill."* Sadly, there was to be no miraculous recovery for Stanley and he died on 12th September.

PORT SUNLIGHT MAN DIES OF WOUNDS.

Mrs. Pearson, of New Chester-road, Port Sunlight, has received the sad news that her husband, James Stanley Pearson, died of wounds in France on September 12th.

"Birkenhead News" report
dated 2nd October 1918.

Stanley is buried in Arneke British Cemetery, where there are 435 Commonwealth casualties from the Great War, a photograph of Stanley's headstone is shown here.
Ethel chose the epitaph, which reads :

*"Till the day breaks and
the shadows flee away."*

Stanley qualified for a British War Medal and a Victory Medal, Ethel also received a Memorial Plaque and Scroll.
He is also commemorated on the Port Sunlight memorial.

As a footnote, Ethel was living at 206 New Chester Road after the war, and the army granted a pension of just £1-5s-5d a week for her and her two children. (£1.27 in todays money) and it wasn't actually paid until March 1919.

330894 PRIVATE ERNEST BARCLAY
9th Battalion - Kings Liverpool Regiment

Ernest was born early in 1896, one of ten children born to Robert and Mary Barclay (both from Birkenhead originally). Robert had always been an Engine Fitter and the family moved from Birkenhead to Port Sunlight in about 1899 or 1900, probably at the time Robert started work for Lever Brothers.

The children were (in birth order) : Robert, Elizabeth Ann, William, Alexander, Harold, John, Ernest, Edith May, Ronald and Kathleen May.

They had been living at 282 New Chester Road, Port Sunlight in 1901 but by 1911 they had moved a few doors away to a 6 roomed house at No. 288 (pictured). Five of the children were now earning their living at Levers as well as the father, and Ernest was working as a Wood Stamper.

There are no surviving army service papers for Ernest but it is,

236

nevertheless, possible to say that he enlisted with the Kings Liverpool Regiment in Liverpool between 15th – 18th December 1914 as 3121 Pte. Ernest Barclay. He was later posted to the 1/9th Battalion with his new Territorial Force number of 330894, arriving in France with the original contingent on 12th March 1915.

It is also known that he fought at the Somme and was wounded at Flers on 25th September 1916.

MISSING.
King's Liverpool Regt.—Pte. E Barclay
330894 (Port Sunlight).

There was nothing in the local papers for Ernest, just a report that he was *"missing"* in the *"Birkenhead News"* of 14th November 1917. As was usual with this type of report it was out of date, Ernest had actually died of wounds on 20th September at the age of just 21.

The 9th Battalion were fighting in the 3rd Battle of Ypres, commonly referred to as Passchendaele, and the war diary gives a good account of what was happening at that time. However, because Ernest died of wounds we cannot be sure what day he received them. The war diary does reveal that the Battalion had been out of the line resting for 5 weeks until the 15th September, and they had not received any casualties.

They were at Vlamertinghe on the 15th, a couple of miles west of Ypres, preparing and equipping themselves for an attack.

On the 17th & 18th they moved up towards the front line, relieving the 5th South Lancashires and the 5th Kings Own Royal Lancasters, with no casualties.

On the 19th they had moved into the front line and were preparing for the attack the following day, but still no casualties so far.

Zero hour on the 20th was set at 5.40am and the men went over the top under a heavy barrage by German artillery, the German positions were strongly defended with plenty of machine guns in concrete pillboxes enfilading the attacking troops. The Battalion advanced in

4 waves, with 50 yards between each. They used rifle grenades against the German positions and were able to advance from shell hole to shell hole, taking more than 60 prisoners in the process. There was violent hand to hand fighting and use of the bayonet at times but the Battalion had soon achieved their objectives. They successfully resisted a strong German counter attack at 7pm, and remained in the line until the 23rd.

So it looks likely that Ernest was seriously wounded in the initial attack on the morning of the 20th and died of his wounds later the same day.

As a matter of local interest John Robinson (New Ferry) and Francis Brady (Birkenhead) were also killed in this action, and on the same day.

According to the war diary the casualties between the 20th–23rd were 6 Officers killed and 8 wounded, and 31 Other Ranks killed, 44 missing & 190 wounded.

Ernest is one of the *"missing"*, but he is commemorated on the Menin Gate in Ypres, one of over 54,000 Commonwealth servicemen who died in the Ypres area and have no known grave. A photo of the panel with his name on is shown here.

He was awarded a 1915 Star, British War Medal and Victory medal and his parents would have received a memorial Plaque and Scroll. His Memorial Plaque is known to be in the safe hands of a private collector of the 9th King's Liverpools, the whereabouts of his medals is not known.

It is believed Ernest's brother Harold served in the Cheshires, suffering a head wound at Messines in 1917 but he survived the war.

30391 PRIVATE RICHARD JOHN EDGE RYCROFT
183rd Company - Machine Gun Corps

IT IS VERY DOUBTFUL IF Richard ever lived in Bebington, his family were usually living in the south Cheshire/Shropshire area. However his mother married a second time and became Margaret Slack, and according to next of kin documents from the early 1920's she was living at No.2 Ash Grove, Bebington.

Ash Grove cannot be traced and perhaps Ash Road near the bottom of Town Lane was where she was living. This appears to be his only link with Bebington.

It is certainly the right man though, the memorial board lists him as Richard J.E. Rycroft and the Commonwealth War Graves have him as Richard John Edge Rycroft.

Richard J.E.Rycroft,   Mrs.Slack,2 Ash Grove,Bebington (mother)

Richard was born in the last quarter of 1881 in the Wrexham registration district, but census records reveal a more accurate place of birth as Shocklach (nearer to Malpas than Wrexham).

In 1891 his family were living near Tattenhall and his father Oswald was a Farm Labourer. There seem to have been four children of the marriage, Richard, Betsey, Mary and Harriet.

On the 1901 census Richard was 19 and working as a Platelayer on the railways. He was lodging in Railway cottages in Chebsey near Stafford.

The following year he married Cecilia Annie Hewitt at Whitchurch, Shropshire and by 1911 they were living at Wirswall near Whitchurch. Richard was now earning his living as a Cheesemaker on a farm.

The couple eventually went on to have 8 children (in birth order) Cecilia Annie, Harry, Richard, Mary, Harriet, John Thomas, Alice, and William Alfred.

Unfortunately Richard and Harriet died in infancy.

The youngest child William Alfred was born in April 1916, about the time his father left for the war. He went on to fight in the second world war and was killed in Normandy on 30th June 1944, a couple of weeks after D-Day.

There are no service records available for Richard and so all that can be gleaned from his medal card and CWGC records is that he joined the Cheshire Regiment initially, as 27505 Pte. Richard Rycroft. He may well have just trained with the Cheshires in the UK and then ended up in the Machine Gun Corps when he was eventually posted overseas, but his medal card confirms that this was not before January 1916.

Richard was in the 183rd Company of the Machine Gun Corps, and they were not sent to France until 19th June 1916 – so this is the most likely date for Richard's entry into the war.

They were part of 61st Division, which had only arrived in France a few weeks earlier (just in time for the Battle of the Somme).

There is no war diary available for the 183rd Machine Gun Corps, and no service record for Richard, so all we can be certain of about him is that he died of wounds on 20th July 1916 aged 34 (or maybe 35).

However, it is likely that Richard received his wounds the day before when it is known that 61st Division attacked at Fromelles. It was a subsidiary action to the major battle going on further south on the Somme battlefield and tragically it was destined to be a major disaster.

The 61ˢᵗ Division and the Australian 5th Division were to be the attacking Infantry, and the usual preliminary artillery bombardment started at 11am on the 19th, with the Infantry attack timetabled for 6pm. However, a heavy German counter bombardment inflicted heavy losses before the attack even began.

After the Infantry went over the top enemy machine gun fire forced 61st Division to retreat without them having reached the German front line trenches. The attack was a complete failure and 61st Division suffered over 1,500 casualties – about 50% of their attacking strength.

The 5th Australian Division suffered far worse than the 61st Division, taking over 5,500 casualties – about 90% of their strength.

The attack was later deemed to have been badly planned, and the official Australian History of the war commented " *It is difficult to conceive that the operation as planned was ever likely to succeed.*"

Richard is buried in Merville Communal Cemetery, just one of 1,262 Commonwealth soldiers buried here.

He qualified for a British War Medal and Victory Medal, and his wife Cecilia would have received a Memorial Plaque and Scroll.

Richard is also commemorated on the Whitchurch Memorial.

LIEUTENANT FRANCIS JACOB SCHENKEL
25th Battalion Royal Fusiliers + East African Intelligence Department

ALTHOUGH HE WAS CHRISTENED FRANCIS, after researching his Lever Brothers and military career it is obvious that he was known to one and all as Frank.

He was born in Islington, London in 1889 (Baptised 2nd October) the first child of Francis Jacob Schenkel and his wife Emily Florence (nee Julier). His mother had been born in London but his father was Swiss.

The couple had married in Islington in the summer of 1888 and were living there in 1891 with Emily's parents. Frank senior was employed as a Grain Merchants Clerk. They arrived in Port Sunlight in 1899, and on the 1901 census they were living at 304 New Chester Road (see photo). The father was working as a Clerk at Lever Brothers and the couple now had their full complement of three children : Francis Jacob jr. Godfrey William, and Charles James.

FRANK JUNIOR WAS EDUCATED PARTLY at the Port Sunlight school, but he probably gained a scholarship from Lever Brothers to attend the Birkenhead Institute. In 1903 he started a 7 year engineering apprenticeship at the soap works completing it in 1910. He had obviously impressed some important people because he was then sent out to West Africa by Lever Brothers to work at their associated company West African Oils Ltd. in the Gold Coast (nowadays known as Ghana). He assisted in the erection of a Mill and buildings at Adjuah.

He returned to the UK in February 1912, but a few months later he was sent to the company's Belgian Congo Oil Works and didn't return home again until July 1914. While he was in the Congo he joined an organisation called the *"Legion of Frontiersmen"* and eventually this was to influence his service in the Great War.

His parents were by now settled in at their new address *"Holme Lea"*, No.1 Oakbank Road in Sefton Park, Liverpool.

Frank's father had moved up the ranks at Lever Brothers and he was now employed as a Translator of foreign languages and was also a Co-Partner of the company. He had been born near the German border in Switzerland so he may well have been fluent in German at least.

The photograph of Frank on the previous page is not very flattering, and another one from Lever Brothers magazine *"Progress"* is shown here, probably in pre-war Frontiersman uniform. After Frank's return to the UK in July 1914 it appears that he was based in Lever's Royal Liver Buildings Office, he also joined the Freemasons in Liverpool in October 1914.

Frank attested as 12880 Private Schenkel to the 25th Battalion of the Royal Fusiliers in London on 15th February 1915, he was aged 26 and his medical revealed that he was 5'-7¼" tall and weighed 10 stones.

The 25th Battalion were popularly known as *"The Frontiersmen"* because it drew a lot of its volunteers from that organisation (mentioned earlier).

After a short period in the UK the Battalion embarked on board H.M.T. *"Neuralia"* at Devonport on 10th April. They were destined for East Africa and arrived at Kilindini, Mombasa on 4th May.

Many readers of this book may be unaware that the Great War extended as far as East Africa, but without going into too much detail here the Germans had a colony there in an area that now includes the countries of Burundi, Rwanda and part of Tanzania.

For the first 10 months of their time in East Africa the Battalion helped to protect the long stretch of the Uganda railway from numerous raids by the enemy.

On 4th June 1915 Frank had been promoted to Lance Corporal and then soon had his first taste of action in late June/early July. He wrote home to his parents on 4th July telling of a successful attack on a German fort (Frank was in *"C"* Company of the Battalion):

"We were away from camp for 11 days, 2 days railway journey to Port Florence, 2 days voyage across the lake to Bokoba, and 2 days battle, returning the same way as we went. Our Company Sergeant Major and one Private were killed in our Company and two slightly wounded - - - "

Frank was attached to the East African Intelligence Department on 4th July 1916, his father may well have taught him to speak German, and this would no doubt have been of great use to the Intelligence Department.

This was no desk job though because the *"Birkenhead News"* reported that he had been recommended for intelligence duties by his Colonel, and it appears that Frank quickly made good, showing *"great ability and pluck in his dangerous duty."* This obviously led to him being granted a commission to Lieutenant in the Intelligence Department on 4th November 1916.

He was on active service continuously for over 2 years before getting a short leave in British East Africa. Not too long after this he was reported wounded at Mahiwa Road in October 1917.

The Battle of Mahiwa took place between British & Nigerian troops and the Germans. It began on 15th October and by the 18th the British & Nigerians had taken heavy casualties and had to withdraw.

Because Frank was with the Intelligence Department it is not known what he was doing at the time he received his injuries. His service record reports that he suffered severe gunshot wounds to his pelvis and thigh between the 15th - 17th October. He was treated for these injuries by B/300 Field Ambulance, but by 21st October he was at 52nd Casualty Clearing Station and he was reported as dangerously ill with Dysentry. Things were going from bad to worse and on 5th November Frank's father wrote to the War Office expressing great concern for his sons welfare. He received a swift reply assuring him that Frank had now been transferred to the No.2 South African General Hospital in Dar-es-Salaam.

However, nothing more could be done for Frank and after a long fight he succumbed to his wounds on 19th November 1917 at the age of 28.

He was buried in Dar-es-Salaam War Cemetery and a photograph of his headstone is shown here.

Frank Schenkel qualified for a 1915 Star, British War Medal and Victory Medal. His parents would have received a Memorial Plaque and Scroll.

He is also commemorated on the Port Sunlight memorial and the Birkenhead Institute Memorial.

Frank's brother Charles served in France with the 3rd Lancashire Hussars and the 7th & 13th Battalions King's Liverpool Regiment.

He suffered an accidental gunshot wound to the knee in 1918 and was awarded a Silver War Badge.

582 SAPPER BASIL HECTOR STEELE
Cheshire Field Company - Royal Engineers

BASIL WAS A NATIVE OF Gloucester, born there in 1886 the eldest child of Frederick & Martha Steele. Between 1901 and 1911 the family moved to Tuebrook in Liverpool. Basil married a widow, Matilda Gertrude Little, at St. Andrews on 18th March 1911 and they set up home at 18 Ashbrook Terrace in Lower Bebington with her 2 children Dorothy & Donald.

Basil had followed in his father's footsteps, both being employed as Engineering Draughtsmen and Basil was working in the Drawing Office at Lever Brothers in Port Sunlight - just a brisk 15 minute walk from home. In 1912 a son Harold Hector arrived, followed by a daughter Brenda Catherine two years later. After Basil returned from the war they had a third child Audrey in 1920.

When war was declared Basil volunteered almost straight away, and joined the 2/1st Cheshire Field Company of the Royal Engineers. Very little is known of his activities because his service record did not survive the London Blitz of 1940, but his medal card tells us that he first arrived overseas on 9th August 1915 when he disembarked in Egypt en route to Gallipoli, landing at Suvla Bay in August 1915.

He seems to have escaped any serious injury at Gallipoli in 1915, and he may have served in Palestine later but this is not certain. By 1917 though he was in France & Flanders. The Lever Brothers magazine *"Progress"* reported that he had suffered compound fractures to his right arm and wrist in 1917 (possibly at Arras) This injury was not actually caused by German hostilities but was the result of a railway accident, the Royal Engineers were required to work on, and maintain, the army's rail network.

Nothing more is known about his war service other than that he was de-mobbed and placed on the army reserve on 4th April 1919. This all looked good for Basil, he had safely got through over 3 years active service and had returned to his old job in the Drawing Office at Lever Brothers.

However, although he appeared to have left the army in good health he went downhill fairly quickly.

On 6th December 1921 he died of tubercular meningitis aged just 36, and was buried in an unmarked grave in Bebington cemetery on Saturday 10th December. (C of E section I, plot 639)
The *"Birkenhead News"* reported on the funeral which was just a family affair and very little mention was made about his war service. His illness does not seem to be connected to the war, and he is not named on the Port Sunlight memorial or on Commonwealth War Graves so it seems surprising that he appears on the St. Andrews memorial.

Basil was awarded a 1915 Star, British War medal and Victory medal.

The family home No.18 Ashbrook Terrace, nowadays No.13 Stanbury Avenue.

93902 PRIVATE GEORGE JAMES POWYS
17th Battalion Royal Welsh Fusiliers

GEORGE WAS BORN IN BEBINGTON in June 1899, one of two children born to William Powys, a Gardener, and his wife Lydia. William was from Pembrokeshire originally and Lydia from Liverpool, it was her second marriage and they were living at 9 Oakleigh Grove in Lower Bebington by 1901 and were still at this address in 1920.

George and his sister Kathleen were at school in 1911 but by the time George joined the army in 1917 he was employed as a Gardener by the Urban District Council.

There is not a lot to tell about George and there is no photograph available of him, but his service record does survive. We know that he was a tall lad for his age 5'-9" with brown eyes and dark brown hair. Although his weight was only 7½ stone his medical noted that he was underweight *"but will improve with training."*

He enlisted as No.2586 with the 57th Training Reserve Battalion at Birkenhead on 10th January 1917, this was previously known as the 9th Reserve Battalion of the South Wales Borderers. He was just 17½ years old.

George was placed on the army reserve at first (probably due to his age) but he was mobilised on 2nd July 1917 and started his basic training in the UK . He went down with influenza on 15th March 1918, and it was serious enough for him to be admitted to 1st Eastern General Hospital in Cambridge, not returning to training until 13th May.

He was eventually posted overseas, arriving at an Infantry Base Depot in France on 21st September 1918. It was at this point, 30th September, that he was transferred to the 17th Battalion of the Royal Welsh Fusiliers as 93902 Private George Powys.

With the benefit of hindsight George only needed to survive 6 more weeks of the war, but just 8 days later he was killed in action.

The Battalion war diary reported that from 6th - 8th October they were in trenches at Aubencheul-aux-Bois, about 10 miles south of Cambrai in France.

The first two days were fairly quiet with just 24 men wounded, but on 8th October at 1am they went over the top. A transcript of the war diary for the day is quoted below :

"Battalion attacked zero hour 1am. Objective Beaurevoir line and high ground in front of Villers Outreaux. All objectives taken. About 50 prisoners were taken. Casualties 10 officers and 120 other ranks."

The casualty figures were not broken down (as killed or wounded) but *Soldiers Died in the Great War* lists 1 officer and 35 other ranks killed on that day, and George was one of them. He was just 19 years old.

George is buried nearby in Prospect Hill Cemetery, Gouy and a photograph is shown here. There are 538 Commonwealth casualties of the Great War buried here.

He qualified for a British War Medal and Victory Medal and his parents received a Memorial Plaque and Scroll.

POWYS.—In loving memory of our dear son Pte. GEORGE POWYS, R. W. F., killed in action in France, October 8th, 1918, aged 19 years. Ever remembered by Father, Mother and Sister, 9, Oakleigh-grove, Bebington.

LIEUTENANT ALBERT DODD
Royal Air Force

ALBERT WAS BORN IN WIDNES on 20th October 1898, the son of Joseph and Anna Maria Dodd. Joseph was originally from Birkenhead and on the 1901 & 1911 censuses he was employed as a *"Marine Engine Driver"* employed by Lever Brothers on their ship the *S.S. Leverville.*

The parents had 6 children, 4 of them surviving on the 1911 census – Robert Samuel, Joseph, then Albert, and William Buchanan. Another son Christopher had died in infancy.

In 1911 the family were living at 242 New Chester Road, Port Sunlight but at the time of Alberts death they had moved further down the road to No. 304 (see photo).

Albert was a very good student at Port Sunlight school and was granted a scholarship by Levers to finish his schooling at the Birkenhead Institute where he excelled in chemistry. He also won a certificate for music at London University.

He had been working as an Analytical Chemist in the laboratory at Port Sunlight for 2 years before volunteering for the Artists Rifles Officers Training Course on 1st June 1917 at the age of 18, getting a commission to the Balloon Section of the Royal Air Force on 1st November 1917.

He served as an Observer with No. 11 Balloon Section in France gaining his observers badge before coming home on leave around September 1918.

Just a few weeks later on 30th October 1918 Albert and fellow officer 2nd Lt. J.A. Carter were sleeping in an old house when a shell struck the building and both officers were killed as a result, four other men sleeping in another part of the house were also injured. Everything possible was done for Albert but he died within 15 minutes aged 20, and just 12 days before the armistice.

Albert was an enthusiastic member of St. Andrew's church, and like his father he was a member of the Oddfellows society - quite how he managed to squeeze so much into such a short life is remarkable.

His older brother Robert had enlisted in the Royal Army Medical Corps on 7th August 1914, and seems to have served right through the war unscathed.

Albert Dodd is also commemorated on the Port Sunlight memorial and the Birkenhead Institute brass memorial which is housed in Birkenhead Central Library at the present time.

He qualified for a British War Medal and Victory Medal and his parents received a Memorial Plaque and Scroll.

Albert is buried in St. Souplet British Cemetery, his fellow casualty Lt. J.A. Carter is next to him.

A photo of his headstone is shown here. The epitaph chosen by his parents reads:

"And soon the night of weeping shall be the morn of song"

THIS POETRY TIES IN WITH the memorial notices placed in the *"Birkenhead News"* on the anniversaries of his death. One of many is attached below.

DODD.—In loving memory of our dear son,
Lieut. ALBERT DODD, No. 11 Balloon Sec-
tion, R.A.F., killed in action, October 30, 1918.
In a foreign land to a lonely grave,
   A sad mother's thoughts wander day by day,
Though alone in sorrow and bitter tears flow,
There stealeth a dream of sweet long ago.
Unknown by the world he stands by my side,
And whispers: "Dear mother death cannot
   divide."
—Sadly missed by his affectionate Father and
Mother, Brothers Joe and Willie, 304, New
Chester-road, Port Sunlight.

446553 SAPPER GEORGE RAMSEY COATHUP
202nd Field Company - Royal Engineers

GEORGE WAS BORN AT SPITAL in the Spring of 1896. His parents Thomas and Ellen (nee Francis) had both been born in the area and were married at St.Andrew's church in 1894. Thomas was a Gardener/ Labourer/Gate Keeper on the various censuses and the family always lived in Lower Bebington or Spital. On the 1911 census they were living at Laburnum Cottage in Spital. Thomas was a Gate Keeper at Lever Brothers and George, who was now 15, was also employed there as an office boy.

There were four children, and in birth order they were George, Margaret, Nellie and Thomas.

George was 18 when war was declared, and he was serving an apprenticeship as an Electrician at Levers. At that time the minimum age for serving overseas was 19, and George didn't enlist until 1st June 1915 at Harrowby Road, Birkenhead, with the 3/1st Cheshire Field Company, Royal Engineers.

Curiously, having enlisted in June 1915, George was not posted overseas until 22nd September 1917. His medal index card indicates that he went overseas to the South Lancashire Regiment at first, but the *"Birkenhead News"* reported that he was with the North Midlands Field Company of the Royal Engineers. It is probable that he was only with the South Lancashires for a very short time and was soon transferred to the North Midlands R.E. with whom he remained until 8th February 1918 when he was again transferred to the 202nd (County Palatine) Field Company.

The German Spring offensive had started on 21st March 1918. This was to be a last throw of the dice by Germany to try and win the war before the American troops (who were now arriving on the Western Front in huge numbers) could help tip the outcome in the Allies favour.

On 24th & 25th April 1918 the 30th Division, to which the Royal Engineers were attached, had been in heavy fighting across the Comines canal and near Vierstraat. There was also a report that the Engineers had suddenly found themselves surrounded by the enemy near St. Eloi (south east of Ypres).

The R.E's own war diary indicates that from 22nd – 24th April Section 4 of the Field Company were at Spoil Bank Dugouts, St. Eloi & Voormezeele, and that they were making preparations for the demolition of two footbridges. At 3am on the morning of the 25th the enemy opened up a heavy bombardment of gas shells. The Engineers wore box respirators from 3am to 8am and stood by all day. From the 22nd – 26th the war diary listed fairly light casualties of : 2 killed, 6 wounded, 8 gassed, and 1 wounded and gassed.

The situation regarding George is confusing, but he was officially reported missing on 25th April at Spoil Bank near St. Eloi. Tragically, his family had still not heard any more definite news of him by January 1919.

It is not known exactly when they did get confirmation of his death, but it was eventually decided that he must have died on 24th April, aged 22.

Not surprisingly in the circumstances, George has no known grave. But he is commemorated on the huge memorial walls at Tyne Cot Cemetery about 5 miles north east of Ypres – and a photo of part of the panel containing his name is shown here. He is also commemorated on the Port Sunlight memorial and on his parent's headstone in St.Andrew's churchyard.

Tyne Cot is the largest Commonwealth War Cemetery in the world. It has almost 12,000 burials (almost three quarters of them unidentified). The memorial walls contain the names of nearly 35,000 Commonwealth servicemen with no known grave.

George was awarded a British War Medal and Victory Medal. His parents would also have received a Memorial Plaque and Scroll.

2156 TROOPER FRANK MELLOR
Household Battalion

FRANK WAS BORN IN RUNCORN in 1875, one of at least nine children born to William and Elizabeth Mellor. William was a Grocer from Cauldon in Staffordshire, and Elizabeth was from Huddersfield. In 1891 & 1901 they were living in Greenway Road, Runcorn and the children in birth order were : Jessie, Florence (died 1893), Frank, Marcus, Thomas, Elizabeth ("Bessie"), Robert, William and Bertram. All the children had been born in Runcorn.

The father had his own Grocery business, and in 1891 Frank (aged 15) was working as his assistant. He continued in this way for another 10 years, and Frank's future looked set to be as a Grocer.

However both father and son were soon to have a change of career.

On 24th October 1906 Frank married Amy Winter at Holy Trinity church in West Derby, and Frank was now living at 41 Brownlow Road, New Ferry. On the wedding certificate both father and son were working as Insurance Agents. By 1911 the parents were living at Ennismore Road near Knotty Ash.

259

Frank and Amy were at No.9 Egerton Road, New Ferry with a 2 year old daughter Elizabeth May. Frank was still an Insurance Agent and working for the Prudential.

Between 1911 and 1917 Frank and Amy moved to 19 Briardale Road, Bebington. This is in the Woodhey area near the bottom of Town Lane and strictly speaking it is within the Parish of Higher Bebington.

There are no service papers available for Frank, and so from his medal index card all that we can be certain about is that he wasn't posted overseas until 1916 at the earliest.

Conscription had been introduced for the first time in 1916, and from June of that year married men up to the age of 41 were required to enlist. Frank was 41 in 1916 and so it looks as though he may have been unlucky enough to get caught by the new legislation?

The Household Battalion were an Infantry unit of the Household Cavalry, and they had only been formed in September 1916. They were attached to 10th Brigade of the 4th Division.

With very little else to go on for Frank we have to move on to 3rd May 1917.

His Battalion were engaged in the Battle of Arras during April and May, and on 3rd May they were to take part in an attack now known as the 3rd Battle of the Scarpe River. Their orders on that day were to capture the cemetery 50 yards north west of Roeux and at 3.45am they advanced, under cover of darkness, alongside the 1st Royal Warwickshires. German machine gun fire from the cemetery and the road south of Corona trench held up the advance and they were forced to retire at 5.30am with heavy casualties. In the afternoon they managed to establish themselves up to the point where Corona trench was blocked by debris. The situation quietened down later in the day.

Soldiers Died in the Great War lists 5 Officers and 93 Other Ranks killed on this day, and other sources give a total of 230 men killed, wounded or missing.

Frank was one of those reported as missing on that day. His wife Amy was no doubt hoping that he had been taken prisoner and she appealed for information in the Birkenhead News dated as late as 21st July, but it is not known when his death was finally confirmed to her.

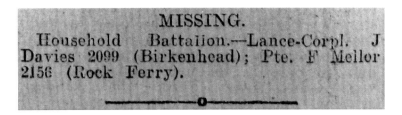

Frank has no known grave, but he is commemorated on the Arras memorial. This huge memorial contains the names of almost 35,000 Commonwealth servicemen from the Great War. These men were all killed between Spring 1916 and August 1918 and have no known grave.

Frank Mellor qualified for a British War Medal and Victory Medal, and his wife would have received a Memorial Plaque and Scroll.

93909 AIR MECHANIC 1ST CLASS
WALTER JAMES DUNN
Cheshire Regiment & Royal Air Force

WALTER WAS BORN IN BIRKENHEAD in the last quarter of 1892, the third of seven surviving children of Samuel and Emily Dunn on the 1911 census. His siblings were : William, Charles, (Walter), Gladys, Norah, Harold & Leslie.

They were living at 36 Bolton Road, Port Sunlight in 1901 having moved from Birkenhead about 1895, Samuel was working as a Labourer in the soap works. By 1911 the family of nine had moved across the village to 38 Central Road but now three of the children were also earning their wages at Lever Brothers, Walter (aged 18 now) was the odd one out, working as a Grocers Assistant in a Co-op shop.

The house in Central Road looks very nice (see Photo) but it only had 4 rooms, and it must have been a bit of a squeeze for them all at bedtime!

Although working in a Grocers shop in 1911 Walter eventually started work for Lever Brothers, working as a Clerk in the Liverpool Branch Office before the war started.

Walter joined the 5th Battalion Cheshire Regiment on 9th February 1916 and probably saw service in France.

He was transferred to the Royal Flying Corps on 26th July 1917, which became the Royal Air Force in April 1918. His service record in the RAF survives (recording his height as 5'-8") and although officially an Air Mechanic it mentions that he was also a photographer.

He was still over in France, near Valenciennes, in January 1919 when he was taken to 57th Casualty Clearing Station seriously ill. He died on the 8th aged 26.

His service record and his overseas death certificate both give the cause of death as *"suspected poisoning."* This must surely have been accidental poisoning, but it would be nice to know more!

Walter's parents received his British War medal and a Victory Medal, and also a Memorial Plaque and Scroll.

He is also commemorated on the Port Sunlight memorial, and on his parent's grave in Christ Church, Port Sunlight.

PRIVATE WILLIAM SPARK

WILLIAM HAS PROVED VERY DIFFICULT to pin down.

The archive papers from the early 1920's regarding the planning of the memorial simply state that he was Private William Spark and he had no relatives in the area. His name had been supplied by *"one of our Storeton district visitors."*

James Griffiths,	Name supplied by one of Storeton District Vis- will try to supply address later.
Michael Hunt,	do. Understand that Mrs.Hall Storeton Hall Cottages, is
Joseph Jones,	do. the only relative of Jos.Jones in the District.
William Spark,	do. & that none of the others have relatives here.

This same Storeton visitor had proved reliable with James Griffiths and Joseph Jones (above) so it is likely that William Spark was associated with Storeton in some way.

There are two likely candidates for the William Spark on the memorial, and it is not easy to get your head around this. To complicate matters further the names Spark and Ellam are both sometimes spelt with an *"s"* on the end. (The variations in spelling are adopted here, depending on the source used).

There was a family by the name of Spark on the 1911 Storeton census, William and Alice Spark, who were aged 66 and 63 respectively. They were married in Liverpool in 1865 and had lived in Storeton since 1871 at least. Importantly, Alice died in 1916, and William died in December 1921. They had 2 daughters.

Elizabeth Ann was born in 1875 and was living with her parents continuously until her death in 1907. Apparently she had never married.

Mary Jane was born in 1870 and she married Samuel Robert Ellam (from the Runcorn area) in 1891. They had at least 3 children, William Ernest born 1892, Elizabeth Alice born 1894, and Rose Victoria born

1897 (she died aged just 1). Sadly Mary Jane also died in 1898 at the age of 28, and in 1901 her 7 year old daughter Elizabeth Alice Ellam was living in Storeton with her grandparents. By 1911 William and Alice just had their 18 year old grandson William Ernest Ellam living with them and working as a Farm Labourer.

It is possible that William Ellam was living with his grandparents from the early 1900's until just before the war, and there was a 11830 Pte. William Ellam who enlisted with the 1st Battalion of the King's Liverpool Regiment in February 1914. He later transferred to the Cheshire Regiment as 33542 Pte. William Ellam, and he was discharged as "unfit" in June 1917. He was awarded a Silver War Badge. A William Ernest Ellam died in Gorton on 11th December 1922 of Malaria, no doubt contracted overseas during the war.

It looks likely that this could be "our" William Ellam (Spark). After living with his grandparents for so many years he may well have been known locally as William Spark? (Remember that both of his grandparents had died before the memorial was finalised.)

The second candidate is 11443 Pte. Thomas Sparks of the 1st Battalion Kings Liverpool Regiment. Thomas was killed in action on 10th March 1915, and he left an army Will. He left everything to *"My loving mother Alice Sparks, of Storeton Hall Farm, Storeton."* He had joined the army as Thomas Sparks but had also noted on the Will that he had been born as Thomas Ellams. There is no birth record for him.

If he had been living with his grandmother between the 1901 & 1911 censuses then perhaps he regarded her as his mother.

With both grandparents dead when the memorial was being finalised, and William & Thomas Ellams being so closely associated with their grandparents, then the *"visitor from Storeton"* could be forgiven for believing that their surname was really Spark, and perhaps even getting the two christian names mixed up. So perhaps the William Spark on the memorial was really the Thomas Sparks who left his belongings to his *"loving mother Alice"*?

With this in mind, the following is an account of Thomas Sparks (*"Ellams"*) death in the Great War.

Thomas enlisted as 11443 Pte. Thomas Sparks in the 1st Battalion Kings Liverpool Regiment. His number indicates a likely joining date of late 1912.

He was with the Battalion when they were posted to France on 12th August 1914, landing at Le Havre the following day, just a week after war was declared.

The war diary reported that they were in billets at Le Preol from 4th – 6th of March 1915, but they relieved the Royal Berkshire Regiment in trenches at Givenchy the following day. The 8th was an *"unusually quiet day"* and on 9th they only had 1 man killed.

On 10th March they had orders to attack enemy trenches from the *"north east corner of the orchard to the Lorgies Road line"*. At 8.10am the attack commenced in 2 columns, "A" Company on the left and "B" Company on the right but the attack failed completely due to the enemy barbed wire not having been damaged by our artillery. They took heavy casualties before being relieved by the 1st Irish Guards at 11.30pm.

According to the war diary casualties for the day were (all ranks) 45 killed, 112 wounded, and 62 missing.

Thomas has no known grave, but he is commemorated on the Le Touret memorial. This memorial contains the names of over 13,400 British soldiers who were killed between October 1914 and September 1915.

At the present time that is all that can be said about the William Spark named on the memorial tablet, but he is surely one of these two men.

If I was a betting man (which I am not) then I think that I would have a punt on Thomas Ellam, who joined the 1st Battalion King's Liverpool Regiment under his *"adopted"* name of Thomas Sparks, being the actual William Spark named on the memorial.

PRIVATE MICHAEL HUNT

IT HAS GOT TO BE said straight away that Michael Hunt cannot be positively identified.

The only clues in the original paperwork for the memorial from the early 1920's were that his rank was a Private and that his name had been supplied by a visitor from Storeton.

Nothing comes up for any Hunt's on the censuses for Storeton, and there is nothing to be found in the local newspapers about his death.

But unusually for what seems to be a fairly common name there are only three men recorded as having died in, or as a result of, the war. Using data supplied by *Commonwealth War Graves* and *Soldiers Died in the Great War* they are :

28244 Gunner Michael Hunt of the Royal Field Artillery. Died of wounds aged 39 in Stobhill Hospital, Glasgow on 30th October 1914. However, he was born in County Mayo, Ireland, and despite every effort on the writer's part no link to the Bebington area can be found.

4436 Private M. Hunt of the Kings Own Yorkshire Light Infantry. Died at home, possibly as a result of wounds, on 17th April 1919. He seems to have been a Yorkshireman through and through, born in Dewsbury, and is buried in Batley (nearby). Again no link to the Bebington area can be found.

10956 Private Michael Hunt of the King's Liverpool Regiment. He was born, enlisted, and was resident in Liverpool but once again he cannot be directly linked to Bebington. But with his local details he is definitely the most likely.

The only other possibility would be if a local man had died as a result of the war between the end of 1921 (Commonwealth War Graves cut off date) and 1923 when the memorial tablet was finalised. Again, no result.

The following is an account of the King's Liverpool man, who may have come to live or work in the Bebington area at some point after the 1911 census.

According to *Soldiers Died in the Great War* Michael was born in Kirkdale, Liverpool, he lived in the city and enlisted there. Commonwealth War Graves also indicate that he was 44 when he was killed in 1915 and that at the end of the war his wife Sarah was living at Salisbury Street, Liverpool. There is a record of a marriage between a Michael Hunt and a Sarah McDermott at St. Joseph's church in Grosvenor Street in 1906 but it is not certain if this is the same Michael Hunt.

However the man we are talking about did enlist as 10956 Pte. Hunt with the 11th King's Liverpool Regiment, and he was posted overseas on 9th June 1915.

His active service in the war was to last less than two weeks, when he died of wounds on 22nd June 1915.

The Battalion war diary reported that they were in billets behind the line in Vlamertinghe from 15th – 20th June suffering no casualties.
At 7pm on the 20th they relieved the Middlesex Regiment and occupied billets in Ypres.

It appears that they were only in reserve and the following day at 8.30pm "A" Company and 2 platoons of "C" Company reported for trench work. Two men were reported wounded, one of them severely. The following day the trench work continued in the same manner with one man killed and 2 wounded.

Michael died of wounds on the 22nd, and it looks as though he must have been the man severely wounded the day before.

He has no known grave but is commemorated on the Menin Gate, a photograph of the panel with his name on is shown here.

Michael qualified for a 1915 Star, British War Medal, and Victory Medal. His wife Sarah would also have received a Memorial Plaque and Scroll.

This may not be the man named on the Lower Bebington memorial, but he is certainly the most likely one.

Unfortunately the mystery may never be solved.

HUGHES D. G.
HUGHES J.
HUGHES T.
HUGHES W. R.
HULME J.
HUNT M.
HUTTON F. R.
HYDE H. E.
INGRAM R.
INMAN A.
IRVINE D. J.

A FEW OTHER MEN

THE FOLLOWING SOLDIERS ARE ALSO worthy of a mention, all of them had Bebington connections and all died in, or as a result of, the war. It should be added that there could also be many others included here, but space does not permit.

LIEUTENANT LESLIE R. A. GATEHOUSE

Regular worshippers at St. Andrews may have noticed a plaque inside the church with this man's name on it (photograph below).

Leslie was the only son of Richard and Rose Gatehouse.
He was from a wealthy family, his father being a Director of his own Brewing Company which was eventually to be bought out by Threlfalls in 1927.
The family lived at Abbots Grange in Bebington before and after the war and Leslie was educated at Eton and Magdalen College, Oxford.

After his education he joined his father in the Brewing business.
He married Cicely Knox in Birkenhead in 1914 (before the war) and they lived at Raby Vale in Thornton Hough, eventually having two daughters Mary Cicely and Nancy Catherine.
He joined the 10th Battalion King's Liverpool Regiment (Liverpool

Scottish) and arrived in France on 4th December 1914. His injuries were received at Givenchy, France in April 1918 and he never fully recovered from them. He died in Carlisle after an operation connected with these injuries on 3rd October 1926 and had a very impressive funeral at St. Andrew's, Bebington, on Wednesday 6th October 1926.

It is ironic that had he died a few years earlier then there is little doubt he would have been named on the memorial.

W/1115 PRIVATE JAMES OWENS

James was born in 1884, the son of a Higher Bebington man and he lived in Higher Bebington for about 20 years and Lower Bebington/Port Sunlight for nearly 10 years. He worked at Lever Brothers for 15 years and was a Bricklayer when he went to the war.

James married Margaret Emma Jones at Christ Church in Port Sunlight in 1903 and they had 3 daughters Doris Irene, Gwendoline, and Eva.

He enlisted with the Wirral Pals soon after the outbreak of war and he was killed in action, aged 31, on 13th May 1916 at Zouave Valley near Arras.

His story is told in full detail in *"Higher Bebington's Heroes 1914-1919"* but it is a long standing grievance of the author that James is not named on either of the Bebington memorials (although he is on the Port Sunlight one).

102207 PRIVATE FREDERICK JOHN BELL

Frederick was born in Birkenhead about 1892, his father was an Assistant Head Postmaster there but by the early 1920's the family were living at *"Malvina"* Heath Road, Lower Bebington.

Frederick was a Plumber and enlisted with the Kings Liverpool Regiment, serving overseas with them initially before being transferred to the 2nd Battalion Sherwood Foresters.

Whilst on active service he contracted an illness which resulted in his death on 5th May 1921 aged 29. He is named on Commonwealth War Graves so his illness must have been deemed to be as a result of serving in the war.

He is buried in St. Andrew's churchyard in a family plot.

Given that his parents were living in Heath Road and that he is buried in the churchyard it seems surprising that he is not named on St.Andrew's memorial. He is not on the Birkenhead memorial either.

DEATHS IN DATE ORDER

31st October 1914	Ernest Watson
13th January 1915	Matthew Fray
25th January 1915	Percy Kendall
18th April 1915	Reginald Davies
7th June 1915	Herbert Dillon
18th June 1915	Frank Smith
22nd June 1915	Walter Severn
22nd June 1915	Michael Hunt (probably)
27th October 1915	James Griffiths
1st December 1915	Kenneth Ford
5th April 1916	George Scheers
28th April 1916	William Forsey
2nd May 1916	Arthur Margerison
14th May 1916	Andrew Dillon
21st May 1916	Joseph Jones
5th June 1916	Henry Smedley
1st July 1916	Frank Davies
1st July 1916	Henry Hughes
1st July 1916	Percy Parry
3rd July 1916	Roland Green
7th July 1916	Frederick Dellow
20th July 1916	Richard Rycroft
25th July 1916	Richard Scholefield
3rd August 1916	George Inskip
31st August 1916	Thomas Gates
23rd October 1916	John Dawber
23rd October 1916	William Wooliscroft
4th November 1916	Philip Shone
9th January 1917	Herbert Suckley
9th April 1917	John Lewis
19th April 1917	Ernest Smith
3rd May 1917	Frank Mellor
10th May 1917	Joseph Mullray
16th May 1917	Ralph Brocklebank
7th June 1917	John Ward
7th June 1917	George Cooper

8th June 1917	Herbert Brown
16th July 1917	Joseph Dutton
19th July 1917	Harry George
1st August 1917	Arthur Nevitt
20th September 1917	Ernest Barclay
3rd October 1917	John Statham
18th October 1917	Ralph Williams
21st October 1917	Arnold Draper
27th October 1917	John Hull
19th November 1917	Frank Schenkel
4th February 1918	Aaron White
21st March 1918	Frederick Hardwick
24th March 1918	Samuel White (Lancaster)
27th March 1918	Percy Williams
3rd April 1918	Eric Davies
4th April 1918	George Whitehead
12th April 1918	James Iveson
24th April 1918	George Coathup
29th April 1918	Alfred Evans
26th June 1918	Horace Holden
6th July 1918	John Gee
12th July 1918	William Brown
2nd August 1918	William Brayne
19th August 1918	William Fitton
21st August 1918	James Smith
31st August 1918	Richard Nicholson
12th September 1918	Stanley Pearson
29th September 1918	Herbert Wilson
8th October 1918	George Powys
19th October 1918	Arthur Davies
22nd October 1918	Ernest Leather
23rd October 1918	Henry Davies
30th October 1918	Albert Dodd
18th January 1919	Walter Dunn
30th January 1919	Norman Austin
6th December 1921	Basil Steele
Not confirmed	William Spark

SOME STATISTICS

(THE FOLLOWING STATISTICS ARE BASED solely on the 71 positively identified names on the memorial)

This book contains photographs for 57 of the men.

Of the 73 men named on the memorial, 38 are also named on the Port Sunlight memorial. Almost all of these 38 men were working at Lever Brothers at the outbreak of war.

The worst affected parts of Lower Bebington were :
New Chester Road, Port Sunlight – 7 men killed.
The Village, Lr. Bebington – 6 men killed.
Bromborough Road, Lr. Bebington – 4 men killed.
Greendale Road, Port Sunlight – 4 men killed.
Oakleigh Grove, Lr. Bebington – 4 men killed.
Trafalgar Drive, Lr. Bebington – 3 men killed.

Ages of men killed :
Up to 19 years - 13
20-29 years   - 37
30-39 years   - 18
40 and over   - 3   Average age of all 71 : 26 years 1 month

Most are from the Infantry, but there are also men from the Cavalry, Artillery, Royal Navy, Merchant Marine, & Royal Flying Corps/R.A.F. The most deaths by Regiment were (predictably) 20 in the Cheshires and 11 in the King's Liverpool.

Proving what a World War it truly was, these men from Bebington are buried in places as far afield as the UK, France, Belgium, Germany, Italy, Turkey (Gallipoli), Iraq, Tanzania (East Africa), Pakistan, and three of them at sea.

Herbert Suckley and Walter Severn are buried locally in St.Andrew's churchyard, John Dawber and Frank Smith are in Bebington cemetery (the first three have C.W.G.C. headstones) and Horace Holden is in a family plot at Christ Church, Port Sunlight. Please pay them a visit, they deserve to be remembered !

SOURCES OF INFORMATION

The *"Birkenhead News"* & *"Birkenhead Advertiser"* from 1914-1921
Wirral Archives.
Port Sunlight Museum Archives.
National Archives
Documents relating to the planning of the memorial, held in Chester
Archives.
Bebington Library.
Regimental or Battalion War Diaries.
"Ancestry"
The *"Great War Forum."*
The Commonwealth War Graves Commission.

BIBLIOGRAPHY

"19th Century Bebington Parish and St. Andrew's Church" by Alan
Roberts.

Countless other books about the Great War, too numerous to mention
here, but occasionally mentioned within individual stories.

HELPERS

I would also like to thank the following people for their help, and encouragement :

Judith Beastall, secretary of the Western Front Association (Merseyside Branch) for so much help, with war diaries in particular.

Peter Threlfall, chairman of the Western Front Association (Merseyside Branch) for help with 13th Battalion Cheshire Regiment in particular.

Pat Pritchard for much genealogical help, and for finding Wilson & Spark.

Joe Devereux for help with the King's Liverpool Regiment.

Stuart Irwin at Port Sunlight Museum Archives.

The *"Birkenhead News"* for allowing me to reproduce some photos and extracts.

People too numerous to mention on the *"Great War Forum"*.

And to my wife Pam for putting up with my compulsive research for more than two years, resulting in the consequent neglect of some household chores.

FINAL THOUGHTS

I HAVE THOROUGHLY ENJOYED WRITING both of my books.

They contain the details and courageous deeds of 106 men from all parts, and fringes, of Bebington who gave their lives in the Great War. I am also very hopeful that with the centenary rapidly approaching more local people will take an interest in the events of 100 years ago, which may result in these brave men being better remembered locally. Their stories certainly deserve to be heard.

If any readers interested in family history would like more information on these or any other Bebington, Port Sunlight, New Ferry, Bromborough Pool or Storeton men in the Great War then please feel free to get in touch. I do have a lot of information about other men from these communities who are not included in this book.

Dave Horne, October 2013.
Tel. 0151 608 7349